T0336344

Obliged to Help

Obliged to Help

Adolphine Fletcher Terry
and the Progressive South

Stephanie Bayless

**Butler
Center
Books**

LITTLE ROCK, ARKANSAS

Butler Center Books	The Butler Center for Arkansas Studies
	Central Arkansas Library System
	100 Rock Street
	Little Rock, AR 72201
	www.butlercenter.org

First edition: September 2011

ISBN (13-digit): 978-1-935106-32-6 (hardcover)

Project manager: Rod Lorenzen
Copyeditor: Ali Welky
Book design: H. K. Stewart
Front cover photograph: Adolphine Fletcher Terry; 1910. Courtesy of the
    Butler Center for Arkansas Studies.

Library of Congress Cataloging-in-Publication Data

Bayless, Stephanie, 1983-
  Obliged to help : Adolphine Fletcher Terry and the Progressive South / by
Stephanie Bayless; also includes photographs. -- 1st ed.
    p. cm.
  Includes bibliographical references and index.
  ISBN 978-1-935106-32-6 (hardcover : alk. paper)
  1. Terry, Adolphine Fletcher, 1882-1976. 2. Upper class women--Arkansas--
Biography. 3. Women--Arkansas--Biography. 4. Women political activists--
Arkansas--Biography. 5. Women social reformers--Arkansas--Biography. 6. Social
justice--Arkansas--History--20th century. 7. Social justice--Southern States--
History--20th century. 8. Arkansas--Social conditions--20th century. 9. Southern
States--Social conditions--20th century. 10. Arkansas--Biography. I. Title.

F411.T37B39 2011
976.7'053092--dc23
[B]

                                    2011017879

Printed in the United States of America
This book is printed on archival-quality paper that meets requirements of the
American National Standard for Information Sciences, Permanence of Paper,
Printed Library Materials, ANSI Z39.48-1984.

For Olivia and Carder,
who were *almost* always patient

Table of Contents

Acknowledgements

First, I would like to thank Dr. Johanna Miller Lewis for planting the idea of this project in my head. Without her offhand remark about the existence of the Terry manuscript and her guidance in organizing my thoughts throughout the project, I would not have completed what you are now reading. You have been a wonderful advisor and a good friend, thank you for your support.

I am also indebted to Dr. C. Fred Williams and Laura Miller, who each brought their own unique interpretation to my research and made it better in the process. Thank you for helping me to see the things I had left out and the things I did not realize were there.

I would like to thank the staff of the Arkansas History Commission and the Butler Center for Arkansas Studies for pointing out undiscovered resources and tracking down obscure works. I would particularly like to thank the staff of the Archives and Special Collections in the Ottenheimer Library of the University of Arkansas at Little Rock for bearing with me as I inspected every single paper in the Fletcher-Terry Papers. Your smiles remained regardless of the number of boxes I requested, and you made my long days of research a little more bearable.

Lastly, I would like to thank my friends and family for their love, support, and willingness to listen. Thank you to Olivia, my little cheerleader. And a special thank you to my husband and mother, who were unable to escape my stories, complaints, and excitement. You listened intently, and you always sounded like you cared and were committed to the outcome. Thank you.

Introduction

At the fifty-ninth annual meeting of the Arkansas Historical Association in 2000, scholars of Arkansas history gathered in Springdale, Arkansas. During this meeting, the group participated in a "Millennium Poll" and created a list of the fifteen most significant individuals who made an impact on Arkansas.[1] Some individuals on the list, such as former president William Jefferson Clinton, were recognizable to many in and out of the state. Others were not as familiar to the general public; one of these was Adolphine Fletcher Terry. Despite the unfamiliarity of her name to much of the population of Arkansas, Terry is well known to historians and scholars. The Arkansas Historical Association poll was not her first appearance on such a list. In the December 31, 1999, issue of the *Arkansas Times*, for example, Robert McCord recognized Terry as one of twelve runners-up to its list of twenty Arkansans of the Century.[2] It seems unusual, then, that a woman of such influence in Arkansas remains largely unknown in the larger scheme of history, particularly Arkansas history. Mention the name Adolphine Fletcher Terry to people you meet on the streets of Little Rock, Arkansas, and their response will likely be a blank stare; mention the events in which she was a driving force, however, and receive instant recognition.

After Terry's death in 1976, the *Arkansas Gazette* called her "one of Arkansas's premier citizens and a lifelong fighter for human rights, racial equality and public education."[3] Her list of accomplishments in Arkansas is long and includes organizing, or helping to organize, the School Improvement Association (a forerunner of the modern Parent Teacher Association or PTA), the College Club (a forerunner of the Little Rock Branch of the American Association of University Women), the first Pulaski County Juvenile Court, the Girls Industrial School in Saline County, the Community Chest (a forerunner of the

11

United Way), the Little Rock Housing Authority, the College Station Head Start Program and Community Center, the Little Rock Women's City Club, the Arkansas State Festival of Arts, the Pulaski County Tuberculosis Association, and the Women's Emergency Committee to Open Our Schools (formed in the wake of the Central High desegregation crisis of 1957). She served as a board member of the Little Rock Public Library, the Pulaski County Juvenile Court, the Pulaski County Tuberculosis Association, the Family Service Agency, the Salvation Army, the Community Chest, the Civic Music Association, and the State Opera Association. She served as an advisory committee member during the formation of the Phyllis Wheatley Branch of the YWCA (the African-American branch located in Little Rock). She was instrumental in the development of a free library system in Arkansas, serving as president of the M. M. Eberts American Legion Auxiliary Post and later as president of the Arkansas American Legion Auxiliary. She served as chairman of the Arkansas State Festival of the Arts, United Nations chairman of the Federation of Women's Clubs, and delegate to the Democratic National Convention, in addition to being named Little Rock Woman of the Year, Arkansas Mother of the Year, and one of Vassar College's 100 distinguished graduates.[4]

In a speech given at an Arkansas Council on Human Relations dinner in honor of Terry, Harry Ashmore explained Terry's impact on Arkansas:

> Education ... is the lodestone of her interests, but her commitment is by no means exclusive. She is a formidable figure in the Episcopal church, and in all the cultural affairs of the city and state; her imprint can be found on every major charitable organization and upon the public welfare agencies ... her unmistakable competence brought her to membership on the boards of all the major charities and civic enterprises, and there she functioned as an early-day ombudsman ... it is evident that she went forth not only to heal but to lift up.

He continued with his analysis of Terry:

> She has shown us the absurdity of so much we believed to be true, and the falsity of so many of our inherited fears. ... Under conditions far more adverse than any white Southerner will ever know again she simply set aside the spurious considerations of race and opened her heart to all those who lived around her. Her operating assumption is that most of us, black or white, are better than we usually have a chance to be.[5]

Despite her significant role in Arkansas history, little scholarly work has been published on Terry's life and activities. *Arkansas Biography: A Collection of Notable Lives* and the online *Encyclopedia of Arkansas History & Culture* both have biographical entries on Terry.[6] The entries touch on the basics of Terry's life from her birth in 1882 to her death in 1976, including a short summary of her family history. While these sources offer an introduction to Terry, the most comprehensive study of her life, "Life is My Song, Also," was written by Terry herself (as dictated to Carolyn Rose) and remains unpublished, but available in multiple Arkansas archives. Named after her brother John Gould Fletcher Jr.'s autobiography, *Life is My Song*, Terry's manuscript offers a wealth of information from Terry's own point of view but lacks detail on the events and issues seen in a majority of scholarly research.[7] Terry dictated her autobiography to Carolyn Rose in 1973 when she was ninety-one years old on the suggestion of Irene Samuel. In a letter to Terry's son describing the process, Rose reveals that she recorded conservations with Terry that did not follow a particular outline and that she attempted to refresh Terry's memory when necessary with information from the *Arkansas Gazette* and secondary historical sources. Later, Rose arranged the information into chapters, adding transitions and making clarifications to the information. It is not known what information Rose might have unwittingly influenced by her personal knowledge or bias.[8] The manuscript starts with a short history of the Fletcher family beginning with their arrival in America in 1840 and then covers Terry's life from her birth in 1882 to her work with the Women's Emergency Committee in 1958. Throughout the work, Terry offers insights into her everyday life in Little Rock, as well as her opinions on family life, race relations, class issues, and religion.

Terry's most documented contribution to society is her role in the formation and activities of the Women's Emergency Committee to Open Our Schools (WEC) during the Central High crisis in Little Rock, Arkansas. In books written by Terry's colleagues from the WEC—*The Embattled Ladies of Little Rock* by Vivion Lenon Brewer and *Breaking the Silence* by Sara Alderman Murphy—the goals and actions of the WEC are heavily documented, and both authors dedicate a section of each book to biographical information on Terry and her role as an activist in Arkansas.[9] Outside of these accounts, information on Terry and the WEC can be found in the official papers of the Women's Emergency Committee located at the Arkansas History Commission and in numerous other scholarly works such as *The Little Rock Recall Election* by Henry Alexander, "Power From the Pedestal: The Women's Emergency Committee and the Little Rock School Crisis" by Lorraine Gates, and *Turn Away Thy Son: Little Rock, the Crisis That Shocked the Nation* by Elizabeth Jacoway.[10]

Although few sources are available that deal specifically with Adolphine Fletcher Terry, a multitude of sources exist that portray women's activism in general and, more specifically, southern women activists. For example, *White Political Women: Paths From Privilege to Empowerment* by Diane Fowlkes, *Southern Strategies: Southern Women and the Woman Suffrage Question* by Elna C. Green, and *Throwing Off the Cloak of Privilege: White Southern Women Activists in the Civil Rights Era* edited by Gail S. Murray all study the motivations and actions of women in various social movements.[11] Articles such as "Diversity Within A Racial Group: White People in Little Rock, 1957–1959" by David L. Chappell, "Arkansas Women: Their Contributions to Society, Politics, and Business, 1865–1900" by Janie Synatzske Evins, and "The New Woman as Club Woman and Social Activist in Turn of the Century Arkansas" by Frances Ross all study the unique situation of Arkansas woman, particularly white women, as they struggle to find a place in society and reconcile the expectations of others with their own aspirations.[12]

Using the sources listed above, as well as other similar works including the extensive Fletcher-Terry Family Papers available at the University of Arkansas at Little Rock Archives and Special Collections, I will look at the motivations behind the activism of Terry to answer the question, "Who is Adolphine Fletcher Terry?" An article in the *Arkansas Gazette* once described Terry as "one of those that people regard as paradoxical, for she was an aristocrat magnificently concerned with the needs and cares of the deprived and down-trodden."[13] By looking at Terry's life as recorded in her unpublished manuscript, "Life is My Song, Also," as well as additional primary and secondary sources by Terry and others, I examine how the daughter of a Confederate soldier and local aristocratic matron became a devoted social activist for multiple groups of all races. The reader will see that Terry had a variety of motives behind her social activism ranging from boredom to perceived obligations due to class and social status to an overwhelming interest in the well-being of those around her. Adolphine Fletcher Terry was in many ways a stereotypical southern aristocrat, but she was also a strong and intelligent woman who was committed to creating a more egalitarian world for those Arkansans who were not in a position to help themselves.

Chapter 1

Childhood through Vassar College

The oldest of three children, Adolphine Fletcher was born on November 3, 1882, in Little Rock, Arkansas, to parents John Gould Fletcher, a Confederate veteran, and Adolphine Krause Fletcher, the daughter of proud German immigrants. Freiderika Haberman, Terry's grandmother, immigrated to the United States from Hanover, Germany, with her brother in 1840. Haberman married John Krause, a merchant from Little Rock, and the couple had four children before Krause's death, after which Freiderika took in the orphaned daughter of family friends, Adeline.[1] According to Terry, her grandparents "gave all four of [their] daughters very Germanic names. Although two of them were not too awful. There was Clara, which is a nice name in any language, and then Johanna, which begins to be a bit strange. Then came Loudovica, which was the feminine for Ludwig, and finally my mother, Adolphine, who was named for her grandfather, Simon Adolph."[2]

The Fletchers were long-time Arkansas residents, with John Fletcher educated in a rural school in Saline County. He served in the Confederate army during the Civil War and was wounded and captured at the Battle of Murfreesboro in 1863. Although he left military service as a major, many people called him "Colonel Fletcher" throughout his life.[3] After the war, Fletcher started buying and selling cotton with Austrian immigrant Peter Hotze.[4] Fletcher and Hotze proved to be successful in this endeavor and continued to expand their business. This was in large part due to the reputations of both men as honest and hardworking. For example, men doing business with Fletcher and Hotze sometimes treated the business as a makeshift bank—"they would bring their money and put it in [Fletcher's] desk with a label indicating who it belonged to, and it would remain safe while they added to it, or borrowed from it as they needed to."[5]

Fletcher's American citizenship, lost after his service to the Confederacy, was restored in 1873, and he was elected as mayor of Little Rock in 1875.[6] Shortly after this, in September of 1876, Fletcher married Adolphine Krause in New York.[7] Prior to her marriage, Adolphine Krause had dropped out of school to raise her siblings while her mother was ill, effectively giving up her pursuit of a possible career in music.[8] Perhaps in part because of this turn of events, Adolphine Krause Fletcher became committed to providing her children with the best education and giving them what she was unable to have, even attempting to interest her son, John Gould Fletcher Jr., in a musical career. In many cases, she was overprotective of the children, including Adolphine, and "unmistakably withdrew from [John Gould Fletcher Jr.] when he proved too clumsy to master the piano."[9] Adolphine remembered her mother as one who "believed in discipline," like most parents of the time, with a number of "idiosyncrasies" such as thinking the "ground was always damp" despite weather conditions or keeping a close watch on her children to prevent their imminent kidnapping.[10] Adolphine Krause Fletcher also tended to overdress her children "both in summer and in winter. [John Gould Fletcher Jr.] in the summer wore kilted costumes made out of Marseilles, a heavy cotton fabric. He was a thin child, and in the summer he would have a heat rash all over his arms, but the amount of clothing he wore remained the same."[11] In spite of her "idiosyncrasies," Adolphine Krause Fletcher taught five-year-old Adolphine her first "lesson in justice" and unknowingly influenced

Terry's later commitment to civil rights. While a cousin, Molly Fletcher, was visiting the family, her diamond ring mysteriously disappeared. According to Terry, the cousin

> had been thinking the situation over, and she was perfectly sure that Fred, the black boy who worked for us, had stolen the ring ... and she wanted my mother to send for the police and have him arrested. My mother refused. ... Fred, she felt, was entirely honest, or, if he wasn't entirely honest, at least he wouldn't steal from us, and the ring must be on the place somewhere. ... As we walked around the yard ... Molly [found] the ring ... in the bottom flounce of her dress. She was delighted to find it, and immediately forgot the fact that she had been accusing Fred unjustly.[12]

Terry describes the effect this incident had on her, even as a young child:

> But I never forgot that particular incident. I had already come to recognize the fact that black people had very little chance to hold their own in an argument with a white person. I visualized what it would have done to Fred ... if he had been taken off to jail. ... In all of my life, I think I have never accused anybody of taking anything. ... The effect it would have on a person's morale, even if the person were proved to be entirely innocent, made me form this resolve which I have lived up to all my long life.[13]

This early incident in Terry's life illuminated the circumstances of the plight of an African American in late nineteenth-century America. As a young child, Terry recognized the unequal treatment of the races, but, while being raised in a community where discrimination against non-white races was the expected norm, did not necessarily believe a change was needed. An event later in life would cause Terry to rethink the southern position on race, but at the time of the incident with the diamond ring, the young Terry is concerned with the feelings of a familiar human being, with little regard for race. This interest in the well-being of all those around her would be a driving factor in Terry's later social activism.

Growing up in Little Rock near the turn of the century, Adolphine lived in an area experiencing economic and social growth. The population of the capital city of Little Rock grew from 13,138 in 1880 to 38,307 by 1900, and the new ideas that would take root in the early twentieth century were beginning to materialize.[14] Unlike their rural counterparts, the Fletcher family was economically strong and had the ability to offer its children the opportunity to attend school and enjoy a childhood without the responsibility of harvesting the crop or caring for other family members. When remembering her early childhood, Adolphine Fletcher Terry explained: "We naturally lived very simple lives then, using what was around us, and making most of our own entertainment. My parents were both very interested in public affairs and read the newspaper daily. … Dresses and underwear, coats and stockings were all made in the home, and most families had a black woman who came in twice a year to help the woman of the house with the sewing."[15]

She elaborated on the particular circumstances of young girls during this time:

> Girls also weren't allowed to play games like baseball because that would make their hands rough and their knuckles large. … Altogether, women's lives were quite different from what they are now. If there were enough money in the family then, the daughters were sent away for a year or two to a finishing school where they learned French, even if they were not ever going to speak a word of French in their lives. And of course they took courses in English and music and learned to paint and do art-needlework, all nice ladylike occupations. Women for the most part were not interested in nor taught about what was happening in the world outside. A few were interested, but most were not; they accepted life just as it was.[16]

In 1889, John Gould Fletcher Sr. moved his family into the imposing former home of Albert Pike located at 411 East Seventh Street. Prior to the Fletcher family's occupation of the home, it served as the location of the Arkansas Female College, which was operated by Adolphine Fletcher Terry's aunt. The Fletcher family made many

improvements to the home, which was built in 1840 and was some-
what rundown after being empty for a few months. For example, soon
after the family moved in, two buildings that had served as classroom
and kitchen space were taken down, and a conservatory, porch, and
indoor kitchen were added. More extensive remodeling was done in
later years. While living in this home, Adolphine interacted with several African-American workers. A number of the wealthy families of
Little Rock employed a light-skinned African-American woman
called "Aunt Lottie" as a type of midwife (it was common practice to
call elderly African Americans "Aunt" or "Uncle" at that time).
Adolphine had a great deal of interaction with the African-American
nurse after the birth of her sister, Mary, who was often ill.[17] She
explained her relationship with "Aunt Lottie":

> Aunt Lottie and Aunt Ples were the two colored nurses who took
> care of all the "quality" ladies when their babies were born, or when
> there was serious illness in a family. ... Aunt Lottie was a typical
> house servant of the old school in looks and ways: a small, meticu-
> lously neat black woman, her stiffly starched dark cotton dress
> touching the floor under a white apron, also starched crisply. ... I
> loved her. ... Whenever she came to take care of a member of the
> family, she always cooked me a special breakfast of tiny crisp corn
> cakes and tea.[18]

The African-American janitor at John Fletcher's office, "Uncle
Robert," collected newspapers from around the state and brought
them to the Fletcher home on Saturdays. Adolphine waited on the
front porch for him every Saturday, then spent the afternoon reading
the various newspapers.[19] The family also had an African-American
girl, Cordelia, living with them in the Albert Pike Home. Cordelia, the
niece of Mary Durham, the Fletcher family's one-time cook and nurse,
was two years older than Adolphine and lived with the Fletchers when
her mother was unable to care for her. According to Adolphine,
Cordelia "became a member of our household and was accepted as

one of us. She and I were always in the same grade, although in separate schools, for then there was a white school and a black school. After she graduated from high school, my mother wanted to send her off to college, or pay her room and board at Philander Smith, but Cordelia wanted to stay here and did so until she graduated [from Philander Smith College] and went to Africa."[20]

Adolphine Krause Fletcher described Cordelia as a "member of the household" to a census taker shortly after the girl came to live with the family. Cordelia did chores around the house and helped to care for the younger Fletcher children. She lived with the Fletchers for twelve years until she became a missionary to Africa.[21] Adolphine was closer—physically and emotionally—to Cordelia than she might have been to a typical African American in the postbellum American South, but it was not uncommon for white children to play with their black counterparts. Terry remembers playing with a young black child named Blondel early in life:

> The first negro child whom I remember as a real playmate was ... the daughter of a cook who worked several months for us. ... Blondel taught me a game which we played over and over again. We could stand some distance apart on the lawn and sing as we approached each other: "Walking on the green grass, Dusty, dusty, dust, Fair as a lily, I choose you as a lily," bowing to each other at the end of the line and then backing away. After a number of those bows we would sing: "Give me now your little white hand, Come and take a walk with me." The fact that one little hand was brown and [one was] white never occurred to either of us.[22]

Although it was not unusual for white children to have this kind of exposure to African Americans, it was unusual for a family to take in someone like Cordelia and treat her like a member of the family, offering her not only monetary support but also emotional support. When later remembering this relationship with Cordelia, Terry remarked "perfect [the relationships] never were, but they were natural and human, and were based on genuine affection, and not hatred."[23]

John and Adolphine Fletcher cared about the education of all their children and began teaching the younger Adolphine to spell at age four and read shortly after that. According to Adolphine, "[My mother] thought that before a child could read, he had to be able to spell. As a result, I first, and later John [Gould Fletcher Jr.] learned to spell every word in [Webster's Blue Backed Spelling Book] before we tried to read. It was very easy; the words were arranged in columns and all the words in one column rhymed … then came two columns of two syllable words … and finally gorgeous, many syllable words, of whose meaning I am still not entirely sure."[24]

Adolphine's mother taught her until she started at a formal school at the age of nine.[25] Adolphine originally started school at a local neighborhood institution run by Mamie Harrell, who released the children in the afternoon for a lengthy recess as she napped.[26] When her mother became dissatisfied with this situation, Adolphine moved to the public Frederick W. Kramer School that had teachers with formal training. When remembering her time in the Kramer School, Terry described it as a "completely primitive" wooden building lacking any adornment. She continued: "There were wooden toilets cut in the yard, but they frequently broke down. The water came from a well or cistern, and at recess a row of buckets were put up on a platform with a dipper or two stuck in each bucket. … For heating purposes there was a large pot-bellied stove in the center of the room. … We cooked if we sat near the stove and froze if we moved away."[27]

Despite the "primitive" conditions, Adolphine's grades remained high and she flourished in academics. After finishing grade school at the Kramer School, Adolphine moved on to the public Peabody High School where she took typical classes like English, Latin, and chemistry and started her quest to help those in need. In an effort to assist a failing schoolmate who would be unable to graduate after the sudden death of her father, Adolphine visited a higher-up in the school system. Her argument convinced the system to help the schoolmate pass and allow her to graduate. As Terry later explained, she "felt something should be done. I didn't put it into words then, but I have always felt that it is awful to let people fail in anything, and especially to begin to make failures of them in childhood and youth."[28] This event represents the symbolic beginning of Terry's commitment to the educational advancement of Arkansans. As a woman who desired to have enough money to give "scholarships to everybody in Arkansas," Terry developed an interest in the quality of courses and facilities offered to Arkansas children and the effect it had on their ability to succeed.[29]

Adolphine graduated from Peabody High School on June 2, 1898, and fulfilled her mother's wish by entering Vassar College in Poughkeepsie, New York, at the age of fifteen. As Terry explained:

> My mother differed from most people of our acquaintance not only because her people had come from Germany, but because they had come from Hanover, Germany. At that time, Hanover evidently was a place where people were very conscious of the fact that they spoke the best German in the country; they felt their dialect was the purest German and they were therefore the leaders of the country. That idea certainly stuck to my mother. ... She expected us, as a matter of course, to lead our classes ... and she knew, and I knew, that I was headed for Vassar College. ... My mother had read an article about the college when it opened, and she felt that was the place for me to go, and Harvard was the place for my brother to go, and by heavens, we went.[30]

Matthew Vassar founded Vassar College in 1861 as an institution to provide women with an educational experience equal to that available to men. In his Communication to the Trustees in February 1861, Vassar remarked, "It occurred to me, that woman, having received from her Creator the same intellectual constitution as man, has the same right as man to intellectual culture and development." Matthew Vassar donated 200 acres and more than $400,000 toward the founding and hoped to create an institution with "curriculum equivalent to that of the men's colleges." Established during the "pioneer period for women's colleges," Vassar College was known as one of the Seven Sisters, northeastern educational institutions with quality equal to the Ivy League institutions available for men.[31]

Adolphine Krause Fletcher had very specific goals for the education of her children. After learning about Vassar College in an article on the opening of the school, she made up her mind that Adolphine would attend (similarly, she chose Harvard University for her son, John Gould Fletcher Jr.) and recruited Blanche Martin (the first Arkansan to attend Vassar) to tutor Adolphine. After reviewing Adolphine's scores on the entrance examinations, Vassar president Dr. James Monroe Taylor suggested that she study at a prep school for a year before entering. Blanche Martin spoke up for her pupil and Adolphine's father intervened on her behalf. Dr. Taylor then changed his mind and accepted Adolphine to Vassar with the understanding that she would seek outside tutoring.[32] When Adolphine's brother John had similar challenges while applying to Harvard University, their father was unwilling to speak up on his son's behalf. Under intense pressure from his family, John spent a year at a Massachusetts prep school before gaining admittance to Harvard in 1903. This favoritism for Adolphine over John caused a strain on the relationship of the siblings.[33]

Adolphine Fletcher Terry was only the second Arkansan to attend the prestigious school after Blanche Martin entered a few years prior.[34] Vassar College proved to be very influential in Terry's life and, like a typical college student, Terry matured and developed many of her thoughts about the world during her studies. Terry experienced a life away from the watchful eye of her parents where she could learn to develop her own sense of place and worth in addition to her regular studies. She grew into a stronger person while at Vassar College in part because she was no longer subject to the over-protective nature of her mother. When she first arrived at Vassar, Terry, who had cried easily as a child, was overwhelmed by homesickness and started to cry. She explained that she felt "completely lost and forlorn, with no future, no past, and nothing to cling to."[35] When the same situation occurred a few months later, Terry was too embarrassed to ask her neighbor for a handkerchief and attempted to hide her tears until she regained her composure. In her autobiography, Terry explained that by the end of her time at Vassar, she would have felt comfortable enough to pull up her dress and weep into her skirt, totally unashamed of her emotions.[36] Despite occasional episodes of homesickness, Terry would later remark that "no one ever had a happier college life than I did" and would remember her time at Vassar fondly.[37]

Terry's coursework at Vassar was typical for the time—she took a variety of lecture courses and studied subjects like ethics, history, and astronomy. She was unable to take music and art classes because they were considered special classes available only to honor students.[38] Terry took German at the urging of her mother but stopped it when the class work during the second semester became dull and difficult—"the book was full of long, hard words, and it was about the old times ... which I found to be extremely dull. After that book I dropped German with a sickening thud and never picked it up again."[39] Terry also took French classes at the encouragement of a boyfriend, Walter Abbott, with the same result. She eventually had to take geology to replace the failed French class. That same boyfriend had been interested in the ocean and "sent me [Terry] some books about sea power. At the time, I had never seen the ocean, but I dutifully read the books."[40] Terry was very eager to learn from those around her and was open to their suggestions for her educational and philosophical advancement. She recalled in her autobiography, "During that first year I learned as much from my friends as from the classes I took ... it seems that I got as much of an education by contacting people and listening to what they had to say as from the class work. And, when you think of it, it was the London coffee houses and the Paris salons in the centuries past which were the centers of education, and not the universities."[41] Terry enrolled in a large number of lecture-based classes (these had not been available in her high school). She was so enthralled with these types of classes that she signed up for anything she could get into, once finding herself in the middle of a lecture given completely in French. She couldn't understand a word, but stayed anyway.[42]

In addition to her typical coursework, Terry took a number of classes geared toward teaching the students about "our communities at home."[43] In other words, the classes sought to expose the students to people of different social and economic situations, possibly instilling in them the desire to work for their community. She describes the effect one of these classes had on her:

> I do remember a terrible experience I had in one of them, on a trip to an almshouse. I had never done any social work of any kind, I knew nothing of what was happening in the community except among my classmates, and I had never seen an almshouse. Everyone who wanted to go on this trip went, and as we left the college, the feeling was that it was a lark. ... When we got there we found it to be clean and neat and perfectly acceptable. There was one woman who was having a baby, and she was in a room of her own, with an attendant. We were told that the baby was illegitimate, and that it was not her first illegitimate child. Everything there seemed to me to be so separate from life. This poor young woman lying there having a baby was so different from anything I had seen before that I simply couldn't take it. I left and walked back to the college alone. The whole thing seemed so unhuman, such a shocking exhibition of complete indifference, so cold, so unadorned, so lacking in any really human sympathy. Of course, people who are paid to work in those places, particularly at that time, naturally become hardened to their experiences, but I don't think I ever became hardened.[44]

Terry would remain largely "unhardened" by the plight of those less fortunate. This would be very important later in her life during her high points of social activism when she was unable to look away from inequality in Arkansas. Her exposure to this grim reality really moved her and possibly contributed to her later devotion to the underprivileged as much as her intellectual discussions with her classmates did.

A later assignment in a similar class had Terry planning a typical weekly menu for a family on a limited income while the unemployed breadwinner looked for work. Terry, largely unaware of how to support a family and how the lower class (perhaps even the middle class, although it isn't demonstrated by this assignment) lived day-to-day, determined that malted milk tablets were the solution to the problem. She calculated the exact number of tablets needed to sustain the family members, but changed her mind when a friend laughed at her solution. In the end, Terry created a typical menu with allowances of meat, vegetables, etc. When remembering this experience in her manuscript, Terry remarked, "From what I know of poor people now, I realize they probably would have eaten all the tablets the first day if they had eaten them at all."[45] This stereotypical remark is in contrast to Terry's expanding view of underprivileged communities during her college years, but nevertheless, these types of experiences made an impact on Terry's life.

Terry's time at Vassar set her apart from the women she left behind in Arkansas. Although typical elite southern women like Terry "often expressed interest in politics, they nevertheless remained untouched by many of the politically oriented reform movements."[46] Terry did not fit into this image, however. Since she attended a northeastern college, Terry was not as isolated from outside influences as her counterparts in southern locations. Also, she was not hampered by the limitations of education in the South, where women "lagged at least a generation behind their northeastern sisters in their opportunities to obtain a college education."[47] Vassar, and other women's institutions, had the ability to "provide extensive opportunities to exercise leadership and to promote students' leadership skills (particularly by providing same-gender role models)."[48] Such institutions produce a historically high number of female activists and influential leaders.[49] For Terry, her tenure at Vassar was a "critical experience" that altered the course of her life due to the influence of her classmates on Terry's beliefs about race, class, and humanity.[50] In her autobiography, she singles out one particular experience to sum up the influence of Vassar on her life. Terry was dining with a small group of friends when the conversation turned to "the Negro problem in the south." Terry repeated the common southern belief that "if a black man assaulted a white woman he should be lynched on the spot." She explains the reaction of her friends and its effect:

> [A friend] looked at me with perfect horror, and I can still remember her exact words: "For the sake of taking revenge on one poor wretch, would you destroy the very foundations of law and order in your community?" … I knew she was right. … It gave me an entirely different look, an adult look, at the situation which we faced here in the south. … That was the beginning … of wisdom, and learning not to accept a thing because everybody in the community was saying it.[51]

Terry referred to this moment as the turning point in her life, the beginning of her willingness to treat non-white persons as contributing members of society. Although earlier instances in her life have previously demonstrated her openness to this way of thinking, this is the first moment when Terry recognized the discrimination on a personal level, realizing her part in the discrimination and the unsteady logic of the "southern position." This incident had a great effect on Terry, who would continue to talk about it and the change it caused in her until her death.

Terry wrote in her autobiography, "My life would have been entirely different if I had not gone to a good eastern college, and met the kinds of people I did."[52] Terry is right about this, but perhaps not just for the reason that she believes. As previously mentioned, a northeastern education was often a precursor to a politically active lifestyle and was often much advanced when compared to similar southern institutions of the time. In fact, it was not unusual for the southern aristocracy to send their children to Ivy League institutions.

In a 1999 study documenting the impact of women-only colleges, the authors claim that "women-only colleges have a special ethos and legacy of taking women seriously."[53] This willingness of the institution to "take seriously" its female students, coupled with Terry's newfound freedom and exposure to a wider array of perceptions, contributed to the changes she experienced while at Vassar.

Terry's experience was not a unique one. It is a "widespread and intuitive belief that higher education institutions in general not only change students' academic, social, and career outlooks, but also affect their values and attitudes."[54] Terry entered Vassar as an emotional southern girl, but she changed into a woman with the strength to stand behind her convictions and a growing interest in the well-being of those around her before she graduated in 1902. After leaving the challenging atmosphere of Vassar and returning to the South at twenty years old, Terry struggled with re-entrance into an environment where she "had no ideas about what [she] would do next" and was limited in her choices.[55]

Chapter 2

The College Club and Improvement of Arkansas Schools

Terry's growth at Vassar College was not instantaneous. On the contrary, it was a slow process with many ups and downs. Her uncomfortable reaction to the members of the lower class she encountered on the class outing, for example, demonstrated a remaining prejudice and acute naiveté toward the world outside of her comfort zone. Terry later described another aspect of her innocence and growth process when remembering a relationship she had with a man after her junior year at Vassar. Terry explained:

> [Walter Abbot] was perhaps thirty years old and came from Boston, which to me was almost another world. His job in Little Rock was to persuade the aldermen of the town to vote in favor of a franchise to build a park in the west of town and to extend the streetcar lines. ... He told me that he was to get on good terms with the aldermen, and also to find out all that he could about them, particularly about their private lives, so they could be influenced, or threatened, to vote in favor of this project. At the time, I thought this was a very smart idea, but thinking back on it, I am constantly amazed at how naïve I was. ... But then my ideas of right and wrong were not completely set and I didn't question the morality of his plan at all.[1]

Abbott was Terry's first boyfriend and, despite the fact that their "standards were very different fundamentally," Terry was able to learn and grow from the relationship.[2] According to Terry:

It was all a lesson for me, and the experience of having a beau was a valuable thing. I began to learn a secret that all girls should learn early, and that is the secret of carrying on a conversation with a man, any man. Men love to talk about themselves. A girl may think they are interested in her, and perhaps they are to a certain extent, but they're much more interested in themselves. All a girl has to do is listen to any man, just turn him on and let him talk and he will have an enjoyable time.[3]

Terry used this new conversational skill throughout her life to gain support and attention for her causes. "Carrying on a conversation with a man"—or a woman—and realizing the benefit a slight kindness or even flattery could bring helped Terry through difficult situations. Even in a heated political situation, Terry projected a warm and welcoming, albeit strong and intelligent, persona that can perhaps be traced back to her first experiences with the opposite sex.

After completing her education at Vassar College, Adolphine returned to Little Rock and set out to make a new life for herself in her hometown—"I came back to an entirely different life, but frankly one that was no less enjoyable."[4] Like most girls her age, she immediately entered the local social scene by attending parties and gatherings, dating—it was during this time she met her future husband, David Dickson Terry—and generally remaining committed to enjoying herself whenever possible. In addition to participating in a number of weddings, Adolphine took up riding. She had been exposed to the idea while attending a wedding in California and because a female rider was not a common sight amongst the Little Rock upper class, she sent for a custom riding outfit from New York. Terry explained:

I decided to soften the blow and have a very good looking riding habit made. ... It was what people now call culottes and had a flap of material in the front and back. When I was not on the horse, it looked just like any other skirt, especially when viewed from the side, and it came within three inches of the ground. With it I wore boots, a jacket and hat, and carried a riding crop. I thought it was quite a modest costume and was amazed when I received a most revolting letter concerning the indecency of my attire.[5]

Adolphine did not let this incident bother her, however. She was becoming quite sure of herself and was unwilling to let the expectations of others stop her from doing something she believed to be worthwhile. She later injured herself by falling off of her horse, hitting her head, and breaking her knee. Terry's sense of smell was permanently destroyed by the accident.[6] Clearly though, Terry already exhibited the confidence and strong sense of self she developed while at Vassar. Unwilling to let social conventions stop her from living and enjoying life, Terry pushed the envelope, albeit in a generally unthreatening way.

Terry's first years back in Arkansas were marked by a number of parties with food, dancing, and games. Her name was published as a debutante when she returned and, although this first surprised Terry, she quickly adjusted to her growing social schedule, even taking dance lessons to prepare. As she later remarked, "It never occurred to me that I would be a debutante, but if anything happened, I always entered into it. Sometimes I went too far."[7] Terry threw herself into the party scene. After Terry missed a party for the first time, Terry's mother had a telephone installed in the home, despite her fear of electricity, so she would not miss another invitation. Typically, these parties were catered by Henry Miller, an African-American man. Miller was trusted by the families to plan the events and present a straightforward bill. He was not, however, given any greater respect for his services. Terry recalled one particular party:

> One of the girls who was part of our group was the daughter of an official of the railroad company. She was rather pretty and everyone went for her at first, but perhaps because she was from the north, she insisted on getting Henry Miller a title and calling him "Mister Miller." At the time, that wasn't done at all. Black people might be

called "aunt" or "uncle," but not "Mister." I think this girl lost out because of her insistence on the title; after a time her father was transferred and the family moved away.[8]

This story reveals an everyday occurrence in a typical southern city like Little Rock. Henry Miller was an integral part of the local social scene and had contact with and access to many of the important families, but it was still considered taboo to consider giving him a title. Terry did not notice the injustice of this situation despite her self-described "life-changing" experience at Vassar; she was more concerned with what the woman "lost out" on due to her desire to give Miller the respect she believed he deserved. It is interesting to consider how Terry's interactions with African Americans could remain unchanged while her deeper feelings about the "greater" injustices could vary from her counterparts'.

In addition to the typical debutante-style parties, Terry formed friendships with a close group of friends, including Sue Worthen, Terry's best friend. Worthen and Terry were both daughters of bank presidents (Worthen's father was the founder of Worthen Bank and Terry's father was president of the German National Bank). After the pair wore matching dresses to a party, they were dubbed the "Gold Dust Twins," and this nickname stuck until they married and moved on to their own families.[9] With her developing group of friends, Terry went bowling every two weeks. Although she wasn't very good at the game, she always enjoyed herself. Another source of entertainment in young Terry's life was the Boathouse. The Boathouse was "Little Rock's social apex of the 1880s." It was formed unofficially in 1877 as a place for the young people of Little Rock society to meet for athletics and social events. The Boathouse hosted athletic events such as regattas and social events including cotillions for debutantes.[10] Terry attended these dances but never participated in any of the races. According to Terry, "I belonged to a generation when most girls in this part of the county never learned to swim. Our bathing suits came up to our necks and had long sleeves which really weighted us down in the water. They had short skirts, but under them we wore long stockings which also made swimming difficult."[11]

Historian Francis Ross describes the turn-of-the-century New Woman as "likely to be better educated than average, possibly holding a college degree" and expected to "work in the public arena in an effort to remake the world in the image of home."[12] She expands on the particulars of Arkansas women—"the New Woman in Arkansas found her greatest expression as club woman and social activist" where the "woman's club provided a conservative, non-confrontational framework within which women promoted self-development and community improvement."[13] Upon her return to Arkansas, Terry started the process of readjusting to Little Rock and finding her place as an educated woman with strong leadership qualities. Such a transition was especially important for a young lady because males and females often exhibit different styles: "Masculine styles are typified by aggressive, task-focused, and competitive traits and feminine styles are typified by passive, interpersonal-focused, and cooperative traits."[14] The skills she learned while at Vassar contributed to Terry's willingness to take an active role in her community and develop her activist tendencies. According to researcher Emily Anne Langdon, "Leadership has been a desired outcome of higher education since the colonial period. Many institutions included in their mission statements the development of leaders for the survival of the republic."[15] Vassar College provided Terry "better opportunities to be actively involved in student organizations, to exercise leadership, and thus to improve their social self-confidence."[16]

In her autobiography, Terry looked back on this time of her life, remembered her focus on more youthful activities, and viewed the time as wasted. She described the early 1900s as her "waiting period"; she waited to marry David D. Terry until he was financially stable. As Terry explained, "I waited for a long time. ... I kept up with my friends and had dates frequently. We were engaged for about four years before we were married. Couples then didn't announce their engagement when it happened, but waited until a wedding was around the corner. … It was sad to have to wait so long, though, and I resent those years because they were almost a total loss. Other than the project on school centralization, I didn't do anything."[17] Terry viewed this time in her life as misspent time, underestimating the importance of her work with the Arkansas school system. In fact, one newspaper article recounted a conversation with Terry: "After college and before her marriage, Mrs. Terry contended, her only useful contribution was to help start the College Club, a forerunner of the Little Rock Branch of [the American Association of] University Women. Its purpose was to encourage other women to go to college, but it also provided its half-dozen members an intellectual outlet for stimulating discussions on any subject, also then a rare opportunity for women."[18]

Looking for like-minded women, Terry co-founded this organization in 1905 for fraternity with the small number of college-educated women in Arkansas and also as an opportunity to increase their numbers.[19] As she explained: "Our purpose was to encourage other women to go to college, but the club also was for our own benefit. The five or six members were kindred spirits, and we found we had learned to have stimulating discussions on any subject without anybody taking what was said personally. You can't realize what that meant, for women had never before had that faculty."[20] According to the club's constitution, its official purpose was stated as: "To associate the college women of Little Rock in intellectual and social fellowship and To promote all State and local educational movements." Membership in the club was open to graduates of colleges recognized by the Southern Association of College Women and required endorsement from the board. A second level of membership, the associate level, was an option for women who had completed only two years of college at a recognized school.[21]

The College Club sponsored the Little Rock Federation of College Women (1919–1929) and did scholarship work through this organization. The influence of Terry and Blanche Martin can clearly be seen in the scholarship choices; the organization sponsored two yearly scholarships for students at Little Rock High School—one to an Arkansas college and one to an eastern college. As further evidence of the influence of Terry and Martin, in 1917, six of the club's twenty-one members were Vassar graduates.[22] The College Club reorganized as a branch of the American Association of University Women in 1922 with Adolphine Fletcher Terry as one of the seven charter members. Terry later served as president of the organization.

Clearly, Terry was looking for something more meaningful than her social events, and through organizations like the College Club, she cultivated a network of supportive women. As explained in *Women Creating Social Capital and Social Change: A Study of Women-led Community Development Organizations*, "Women in particular, although denied voting rights and equal status in the political system, were community activists, significantly engaged in building community cohesion" and "women leaders often have networks of women friends who support them personally, and many encourage the formation of these networks."[23] Historian Francis Ross elaborated on this phenomenon, explaining that these organizations "allowed [a woman] to broaden her horizons, gain knowledge, confidence, and skills, draw support from like-minded women, and exert greater public influence than ever before. With strength through organization she transcended the traditional limitations that had restricted her to domestic life."[24]

It was during this time that Terry was involved in her first project as a social activist. Terry and Blanche Martin, who had returned to Little Rock after teaching in a boarding school, were asked to serve on a committee investigating the statutes of the Arkansas educational system. Terry had no specific qualifications for this project, but she was one of few college graduates in the state and this made her a likely pick. Prior to this national committee, the Arkansas Teachers' Association appointed a ten-person committee to study rural Arkansas schools. This committee listed two main problems: "a lack of revenue, which produced marked differences in the length of the school term" and "a lack of efficiency through a useless multiplication of school districts." The committee recommended "a larger taxing unit, as the townships instead of the school district," "a renewal or extension of the constitutional limit on the right of taxation," and "consolidation and transportation."[25]

The Arkansas school system was facing numerous challenges during this time as enrollment grew and standards changed. The state's insistence on maintaining a large number of small schools exhausted funding and strained staff. One historian studying Arkansas schools in the early twentieth century remarked, "The very harmful effects of such a multiplication of small school districts upon the entire education system of the State is apparent to every one at all conversant with the disadvantage of such districts."[26] Arkansans were not unaware of these problems, and the propositions of Terry's group were not new ideas. In fact, the state had taken steps in an effort to correct the problem. In 1903, for example, an official state course of study was adopted by the Arkansas legislature, improvements were made to the teacher licensing law, and the school term was increased to four months. According to the *History of Public Education in Arkansas*, the Arkansas Teachers' Association had already expressed a need for "County supervision, county and State normal schools, and more money to be obtained through a better assessment law." The committee Terry served on was another response to these needs and concerns.[27]

One of the first things Terry and Martin discovered in their research was the lack of adequate supervision in the Arkansas school system. They discovered a system of one-room rural schools that were largely on their own, with some oversight by local school boards but no standardization of rules or regulations. In 1904, Arkansas had approximately 7,000 schools, each with sparse attendance.[28] For example, in 1904, a total of 4,034 schools had fewer than forty-one pupils in daily attendance—104 schools had fewer than seven pupils in daily attendance. In contrast to the number of schools, per capita expenditure for teachers' salaries based on the number of students during the 1903–04 school year was only $3.29.[29] This over-abundance of schools was not a new development for Arkansas. As early as 1880, State Superintendent of Public Instruction James L. Denton voiced his concerns, "There is a strong tendency throughout the State to have too many districts. An undue multiplication of districts leads to a waste of public funds. Small districts necessitate cheap schoolhouses, inefficient teachers and short terms. ... Every man cannot have a school at his door. It is better to have one strong school than several weak ones."[30] Later, J. J. Doyne, superintendent of public instruction, elaborated on this situation and spoke candidly about what he believed to be a great flaw in the local systems:

> The county court has the power to dissolve any school district ... also to form new districts or change the boundaries of old districts, upon a petition of a majority of the electors residing upon the territory affected. The only provision—one which is not always complied with—being that there shall be left in the districts affected, of the new districts formed, at least thirty-five persons of school age. The causes that lead to requests for formation of districts are innumerable, and too often our county courts are inclined to consult the wishes of a disaffected few rather than act as may be for the best interests of the entire district.[31]

Doyne approved of consolidation of districts and bussing students to new districts and supplied ten points in support of his arguments. He argued that consolidation 1) "secures a prompt attendance from the pupils" 2) "increases interest in the school work" 3) "lessens the number of teachers to be employed" 4) "brings about better classification" 5) "diminishes the per capita cost of education" 6) "provides a fund for the erection of better school buildings" 7) "extends the length of the school term" 8) "affords protection to the children against inclement weather" 9) "insures greater regularity of attendance" and 10) "helps to secure better roads."[32]

John Hinemon, superintendent of public instruction from 1902 to 1906, also commented on this situation in his 1903–04 biennial report: "The attempt to put a school at every man's door has resulted in a large number of small schools, many of them taught by young persons who are not fitted by age, experiences, scholastic attainments or otherwise for the delicate and difficult work of training the young."[33] He elaborated in his 1905–06 biennial report: "The meager attendance and poor schoolhouses in many sections are due entirely to these small districts, in which the school funds are so little that nothing in the way of real service can be accomplished and where only inferior teachers can be had at any time. Would it not be wisdom and patriotism on the part of the legislature to take hold of this matter with a strong hand and enact legislation which will insure good teachers and comfortable schoolhouses to all the children of the State?"[34]

The solution was a simple one for the young and eager Terry who believed that "we [Terry and Martin] could solve this problem and do something that had not been done before."[35] This moment of confidence, perhaps bordering on lingering youthful naiveté, shows the stronger, adult Terry who was ready to start her life as an active part of her community and who believed that she had the ability to change the system. Perhaps building on the suggestions of the past superintendents, the confident Terry and Martin came up with recommendations for the school system. Namely, that each county have a superintendent of schools to establish some standardization and that consolidation of schools, including transporting children to new areas, be investigated and instated.[36] Although these ideas were not revolutionary to the teachers and school administrators, these concepts, particularly consolidation and transporting of children, were new ones to the general population of Arkansas.

To spread knowledge and seek support for their recommendations, the women wrote to a number of the leading male teachers in the state asking if they would write three-hundred-word essays on consolidation and the importance of school reform. They chose to contact only male teachers, believing—probably rightly—that their words would have more influence. Through Clio Harper,[37] who was in charge of putting together a section of stories to be sent from Little Rock to numerous county newspapers, the women succeeded in having a weekly article on education distributed across the state. The women edited the articles and cut them down when necessary. In an interesting switch of typical gender roles, David Terry, who was in law school at the time, took on the role of secretary to the women and typed up the articles for publication.[38] They also paid for all of their own materials, including the cost of sending a copy of Among Country Schools by Olly Jasper Kern to anyone who requested it. In Terry's mind, this was a small sacrifice to make for her cause: "I feel that people shouldn't go into anything unless they are willing to give something, money included ... all our expenses came out of our own pockets. ... I doubt if we ever spend a hundred dollars. We didn't commission a group to make a survey, we didn't hire a staff, we didn't spend money evaluating the results or traveling around consulting, but we got the program of centralization started."[39] According to Terry, the first consolidated school opened in Scott, Arkansas, in 1908.[40] While this might have been the first consolidation to happen after their statewide campaign, it was not the first consolidation in Arkansas. In his 1903–04 biennial report, Superintendent John Hinemon refers to recently consolidated districts in Lonoke, White, and Clark counties.[41]

This move toward consolidation and centralization of authority did not happen without some legislative action. In 1874, the Arkansas constitution "fixed a limit of two mills for general taxation and five mills in the districts." This was raised by a 1907 constitutional amendment to three mills for general taxation and seven mills in the districts. The legislature of 1907 also established the office of county superintendent in an effort to centralize authority over the schools. To become county superintendent, a person was required to have taught in the county for at least twenty-four months of the previous five years and to hold a first-grade certificate. The 1909 legislature enacted more laws relating to the state educational system. For example, two compulsory attendance acts were passed and agricultural education was considered. Most notably, however, the legislature passed an act allowing the consolidation of schools. According to Stephen Weeks, this act allowed "the patrols of any rural territory to petition the county court for the organization of a special or single school district having all the rights and privileges previously allowed only to schools in incorporated towns and cities." In other words, it allowed rural areas to establish schools other than the traditional one-room schoolhouses. The 1911 legislature passed thirteen acts related to education and elaborated on consolidation. The new consolidation act allowed two (or more) districts to vote on and carry out consolidation with the possibility of student transportation when necessary.[42] Although the concept of student transportation, or bussing, has since become a negative concept after its use in the efforts to desegregate school districts, Terry was pleased with the work she accomplished during her early work with the school system. She worked on the project for two years and later explained that she found the project easy to do because "the time was ripe for it to happen."[43]

Another outgrowth of Terry's work with Arkansas schools was the School Improvement Association, a forerunner to the modern-day Parent Teacher Association. The first School Improvement Association in Arkansas was organized in Little Rock in 1905. Early efforts of the association in Little Rock were so successful that the Conference of Education in the South donated $1,000 in support of the work. By January 1909, after a campaign started by Superintendent of Public Instruction George B. Cook, seventy-six associations were operating across Arkansas, with 2,256 members total.[44] School Improvement Associations in Arkansas worked to get parents involved in their local schools. They organized school clubs, provided additional scholarly recourses for the classrooms, and worked to beautify and improve school grounds.[45] These associations raised the majority of the funds necessary for their own projects. Their efforts "foster[ed] local pride and serve[d] in a most admirable way to attract and increase the interest of patrons."[46]

Like was the case with her creation of the College Club, Terry's willingness to take part in the school reorganization stemmed from her desire for a project to occupy her time. Secondary to this was a desire to direct change in the Arkansas educational system. This was not unusual for women of Terry's social standing: "Community volunteering constituted the careers of upper-class women. Volunteering was one way in which upper-class women carved out meaningful work outside of the home … and for some, became power brokers in their community."[47] Nor was this type of social work unusual for women in the early twentieth century. Women often worked for causes involving the well-being and education of children because these kinds of activities were perceived to be fitting of their social standing and an extension of their role as women and mothers. Women were able to participate in their communities in a way deemed acceptable. Though this type of "community participation on behalf of children and in support of traditional motherhood provided an avenue for developing skills, networks, and talents … for some women, work centered on children was only a starting point for community involvement in formal politics."[48] This was certainly the case for Terry. This first foray into the world of community participation, although motivated largely by boredom, started a lifetime devotion to social and political activism and, particularly, a focus on the quality of life available to Arkansas's youth, which led to Harry S. Ashmore later describing her as the "midwife and practical nurse for so many of Arkansas's educational intuitions."[49]

Chapter 3

Marriage and Work
with the Juvenile Court

Terry participated in the school reorganization project mainly because, as was typical for a woman of her age and class, she did not have any regular duties to occupy her time. But regardless of the reasoning behind her actions, Terry participated fully in the project and often went above and beyond the requirements, showing an early dedication to the well-being of Arkansas youth. Due in part to this commitment, Terry walked away from the project happy with her contributions to the Arkansas educational system and content that she had filled her time as best as she could. This would be the last time Terry found herself with such leisure time, as family life and outside commitments would soon occupy her days.

Adolphine Fletcher and David D. Terry became engaged during a few days relaxing at a friend's country farm. According to Adolphine, "Occasionally I smoked, and as we sat on the couch talking, Mahlon offered me a cigarette and I took it. Dave insisted that I not smoke it, and took it out of my hands. Well, we had a mild row over that, but before the end of our stay at the farm we knew we would ultimately marry."[1] Although she had found a future spouse who was not critical of her strong will and opinions, the couple did not immediately marry due the wishes of Adolphine's mother, who likely felt she was losing control over her children after John Gould Fletcher Jr. left Harvard

University to pursue a literary career in Europe. Adolphine believed that "[my mother] would have forgiven me had we gone ahead, but I just couldn't take that chance because she was a very stubborn woman and I didn't want to hurt her."[2] Following the death of her mother in 1909, Adolphine Fletcher and David D. Terry were married in the front parlor of the family home on July 7, 1910, after a four-year engagement.[3] He was twenty-nine years old and she was twenty-seven. Terry described the event in her manuscript: "I invited my mother's relatives who were in town, Clara Heidl and Fred Hotze, two friends of Dave's, his father and brother and my sister. ... Just before the wedding Mary rushed out and got some flowers because she thought it was disgraceful to have a wedding without flowers. The news had spread ... and several servants who had worked for my family in the past gathered in the back parlor, so there were really more people present than we had intended."[4] Terry discarded her mourning clothing during the wedding and instead wore a dress that was "white and was trimmed in white crepe, which seemed rather incredible at the time because crepe had been invented to use when people were in mourning and was generally made into veils or used to decorate the house."[5] For the first year of their marriage, however, Terry remained in mourning for her mother and wore black most of the time. After the wedding, the couple visited Hot Springs, Arkansas, and traveled by boat from New Orleans, Louisiana, to New England before returning home.

Soon after they were married, the Terrys were presented with a new business venture—the building of a new department store for Gus Blass and Company as part of its competition with the local Pfeifer Brothers. Both with beginnings in the late 1800s, the Pfeifer and Blass department stores were two of the premier stores in Arkansas. The Terry family had owned property at 4th and Main Streets in Little Rock since 1868. David D. Terry started plans to build the new Blass Building on the site in 1910.[6] Although the Terrys' foray into construction and real estate was ultimately successful, it was plagued with problems from the start. In addition to unforeseen construction issues, the main contractor attempted to commit suicide on the site due to financial troubles. Later, insurance problems arose because changes in the building had not been properly reported. In the end, however, the construction of the Blass Building was a successful endeavor and a testament to the couple's ability to take on projects and achieve goals. The Terrys quickly paid off the building loans and lived off of the rent for many years.[7] The building—designed by George R. Mann, architect of the Arkansas State Capitol—was built in two stages and finished in 1913. It was Little Rock's fifth building of that size and became the first Arkansas store to have air conditioning and an escalator. The Terry family owned this building until selling it to the First Arkansas Bankstock Corporation in 1974.[8]

The Terrys' first child, David D. Terry Jr., was born in June 1911, although he was not the first child in the home, as David Terry's sister, Mary Louise,[9] had been living with the family after the death and sickness of both her mother and stepmother. Adolphine Terry enjoyed her growing family: "I had a gift for taking care of children since they never upset me very much and I could usually think of things for them to do. Dave was very proud of his handsome son, and we did a lot of silly things which gave us pleasure."[10] Notably, Terry set out to raise her children differently than she was raised: "Reacting to my own upbringing, I raised David not to be afraid of anything. He was never told to avoid large dogs or not to climb trees, and he could have slept on the grass if he had wanted to."[11] David proved to be an adventurous child. In January 1915, for example, he took off to explore Little Rock on his tricycle—without informing his parents. He was found two hours later watching the trains at the Rock Island Station. The search for David was extensive enough to be noted in both the *Arkansas Democrat* and *Arkansas Gazette*.[12] Later, Terry was visiting Chicago with her children (three at that time). Overwhelmed by the children and luggage, she left little David on the platform. When the train arrived back at the station to retrieve him, an unafraid David was happily seated on a bench waiting for his mother, never doubting that she would return for him.[13]

As Terry tended to her new family, Arkansas was changing around her during what is commonly called the Progressive Era, a reform-minded time of striving for economic, social, and political justice. Although members of the movement often differed in views on particular issues, historians generally agree on three basic goals of Progressivism—"regulation of business; reform of the political systems and the purification of politics; social justice and the conservation of human and natural resources."[14] In Arkansas, Progressivism appeared in the late nineteenth century and continued to grow during the early twentieth century, but growth of the movement was most challenging in the South due in part to southerners' view of an active government having been soured by memories of Reconstruction.[15]

Historian Carl Moneyhon, author of *Arkansas and the New South, 1874–1929*, describes Progressivism as involving a "new social and political philosophy that rejected a laissez-faire approach and advocated increasing centralization of power at the hands of a strong government" and contends that the movement first took hold in Arkansas in local governments as communities required more services and official support.[16] Reform was needed in the South, and Progressivism increasingly began to take hold, particularly in urban governments. In Arkansas, the state government increased involvement with these local urban governments before initiating its own Progressive reforms under the leadership of legislators Joseph T. Robinson and William F. Kirby, as well as Governor Jeff Davis.[17] The election of Governor George W. Donaghey in 1908 represents the full realization of Progressive ideals in Arkansas and the beginning of a wave of new legislation aimed at increasing government participation in the lives of its citizens.

As the Progressive movement took hold nationally and the build-up toward suffrage continued, American women took advantage of the changing atmosphere to expand their political roles and express their opinions in a more open and honest manner. Women faced a world that "scandalized and oppressed them with economic injustices and corporate wrongdoing and afforded many of them neither longevity nor good health" but still "believed in the possibility of changing it."[18] Progressive causes were particularly popular with women since they often represented avenues that could still be considered an extension of their role as the keepers of America's morality—education and other child-centric reformation, for example—and many women continued to work through clubs as their only avenue of political recourse. In fact, many women's clubs would eventually support the entire Progressive platform through their political and social work. Not wanting to forever be confined to a limited number of causes, women activists fought for their place in a world where they were denied equal participation and continued to be involved in community activism despite their limited and oppressed rights. As a group, women were "significantly engaged in building community cohesion" particularly through women's associations and clubs whose members prioritized the abolition of poverty.[19]

The women's movement continued to push back against the accepted level of political and social activism allowed and tested the socially imposed limits, becoming more visible by 1910.[20] It is important to note that women were not new to activism; in fact, women—organized across class lines—can be found as motivating persons and factors throughout history. Described as the "backbone of collective action," women often performed the majority of the ground work for organizations, whether it was assembling mailers, recruiting supporters, or any number of other required activities.[21] Clearly, Terry is a good example of how women became involved in public issues at the beginning of the twentieth century in a nonintrusive and acceptable way. During this period of Progressive reforms prior to suffrage, Terry took on her next project—her most ambitious yet—and moved deeper into her developing activist life. This particular venture fit right into the Progressive platform of conservation of human resources which, in Arkansas, materialized as labor and state prison system reforms, as well as the creation of measures for the "state's population of unfortunates" including children and people with chronic medical conditions.[22] Success in these measures depended on an expanding role of the state government in the well-being of its population. As Arkansans opened up to the idea of a strong and active government, particularly in urban areas, Terry welcomed a chance to once again work for Arkansas youth.

Arkansas needed an avenue to deal with juvenile delinquents and, as she was always concerned with the well-being of children, Terry was a natural choice to help develop an official Arkansas Juvenile Court. Nationally, juvenile courts were a recent development; the first was established in 1899 in Illinois. It operated under the idea that "children—even children who broke the criminal law—differed from adults" and needed to have separate provisions under the law.[23] Other states followed suit and based their legislation largely on this first Illinois court. According to author Ellen Ryerson: "The creation of the court marked the height of confidence in the possibility of reclaiming delinquents for an orderly and productive social life."[24] The establishment of juvenile courts and reform schools was largely a response to changing attitudes toward social problems, indicative of the Progressive Movement, and a response to the criticism of the current treatment, often inhumane and focused on retribution, of youth offenders. During this time, "reformers also expressed dissatisfaction with the criminal law for failing to distinguish between young offenders and adults, as if they were moral and psychological equals" and "objected to a system of criminal justice and a courtroom procedure which paid no attention to the offender but only to the offense."[25]

In Arkansas, several types of people campaigned for state attention to juvenile delinquents—for example, school officials, some politicians, and women's groups such as the Arkansas Federation of Women's Clubs and the Woman's Christian Temperance Union voiced opinions on the issue.[26] In fact, in 1898, the Women's Co-operative Association of Little Rock drafted a resolution presented at the annual meeting of the Arkansas Federation of Women's Clubs calling for support of a "juvenile reform facility."[27] Arkansas Act 215 in 1911, largely drafted by Minnie Rutherford-Fuller of the local Woman's Christian Temperance Union, established juvenile courts in several Arkansas counties, including Pulaski. The legislation called for county courts to have jurisdiction over the new juvenile courts and for all cases to be handled by the regular county judge without a jury.[28] In August 1911, Terry—along with Blanche Martin and other members of the College Club who had been appointed by the club president to inquire about the progression of the court—went to see Judge Joseph Asher, who was in charge of appointing a probation officer and a juvenile court board. Several days later, Terry discovered that Judge Asher had appointed her as chairman of the juvenile court board.[29] Other members included Elmer O. Manees of North Little Rock, Fannie Mitchell of Little Rock, and Wallace Townsend of Little Rock.[30] Terry was unsure of her ability to serve on the board. She visited Judge Asher and, as she put it, she "told him that I had a young child and didn't really think I could devote any time and effort to the juvenile courts, and besides, I know nothing about it. He said he knew nothing about it either, since it was a new idea, and he was as busy as I was. I couldn't argue with that."[31]

The official legislation, a statute added to existing laws, offered little direction for carrying out the establishment of juvenile courts and left the details up to local authorities. This created a situation in which the local authorities "not only interpret the law but usually have a free hand in applying its provisions." Although the legislation was likely kept vague to allow for a liberal interpretation and enactment, the end result was a very difficult task for Terry and the rest of the committee without a model or resource to consult.[32] The legislation creating the juvenile court outlined the role and requirements of the board:

> The judge of the juvenile court shall appoint a board composed of six reputable women and men who will serve without compensation, to constitute a board of visitation, whose duty it shall be to visit as often as once a year all institutions, societies and associations, receiving children under this Act, and report to the judge of the juvenile court the condition of such children and the manner in which such institutions are conducted; the said board of visitation shall recommend to the judge of the juvenile court the chief probation officer and such assistant probation officers, as may be necessary.[33]

The Arkansas juvenile court law applied to juvenile delinquents as well as "dependent" children and "neglected" children. The law defined these types of children as "any male child who while under the age of seventeen years or any female child who while under the age of eighteen, for any reason, is destitute, homeless, or abandoned, or dependent upon the public for support, or has not proper parental care or guardianship; or habitually begs or receives alms; or is found living in any house of ill fame or with any vicious or disreputable person; or has a home which by reasons of neglect, cruelty, or depravity, on the part of its parents, guardians, or any other persons in whose care it may be, is an unfit place for such a child."[34] Terry, a very hands-on member of the board, interacted with the children on a very personal level. For example, when Terry encountered a teenage girl from a dysfunctional family who had nowhere to stay, she took the girl into her own home, even taking the child with the family on a vacation to Atlantic City. After the vacation, Terry gave the girl a ticket to Nashville, Tennessee, so she could get nurse's training and move on to a better life.[35] Terry was always willing to spend time and money to help those she could and instead of giving the child a few dollars and sending her to a local church or other charitable institution, she went above and beyond what most would do, by attempting to see the situation all the way through. Although she had the best interests of the children at heart, Terry was quite naïve about how to rehabilitate a juvenile: "Somewhere I had got hold of the idea that just by smiling at a child a person could reform him. But a boy or girl of thirteen or fourteen, who is already deeply involved in antisocial conduct, can't be reformed by a smile."[36]

Judge Asher and the committee appointed William Rankin as chief probation officer in 1911 and Netta (or Yetta) Schoenfeld (Mrs. Solomon Schoenfeld) as assistant probation officer. According to the law, the county probation officers were to be "discreet persons of good, moral character" with duties including investigation cases and appearing in court.[37] Terry however, was not pleased with the Judge's choices: "The man who was appointed chief probation officer was given the job simply because he needed work. He was a political appointee who had no real interest in the project. The person who was chosen by the juvenile court board to be the assistant probation officer had worked as a probation officer in a large city and came highly recommended. Unfortunately, this woman had a card index file kind of mind and was not cut out to be an effective social worker."[38] Terry was particularly upset with the choice for assistant probation officer because her strict line of questioning often frightened the children, leaving them unwilling to accept the help that was being offered.

In the early stages of the juvenile court, the board, including Terry, did not hesitate to house the juvenile delinquents in their own homes as part of their families. Although little is known about how this situation was handled, it seems likely that the children would have been required to perform age-appropriate household chores in exchange for room and board. This close contact would also assure the members of the juvenile administration center that the children were attending school and being properly looked after. Eventually, the number of children coming into the system outnumbered the available homes and the board needed to find appropriate housing. As a quick solution to the problem, the board hired Mrs. Missouri Hathaway to live in a probation house with the children. Terry acquired the house from her cousin but did not tell him what she planned to use it for. Unfortunately, the assistant probation officer used the court's Black Maria or "paddywagon" to transport the children to the homes, causing an outcry from the neighbors. Terry's cousin asked her to remove the children immediately, and the board complied.[39]

After the loss of the first housing, Judge Asher gave the committee temporary use of the second floor of the Gans Building located at 614 West Second Street in Little Rock. The Pulaski County Juvenile Court would eventually grow to inhabit the entire Gans Building and contain a school for the children started by Emma Reiman. The probation officer positions experienced a great deal of turnover during this time—Rankin was replaced by Courtney Carrol, who served from 1912 to 1913 before leaving to pursue a music career. Erle Chambers served in the post next from 1913 to 1916 at the urging of Terry.[40] After Chambers left the position and went on to work for the Arkansas Tuberculosis Association, Jennie Dodge, a Little Rock Public School teacher who had worked with both Terry and Chambers during a previous situation with a delinquent boy, became chief probation officer in 1916. Dodge was fully committed to her new title and even studied a juvenile court in Michigan before returning to Little Rock to begin a campaign for support for its juvenile court. After Dodge left the position in 1921, Lillian McDermott, later Arkansas's first certified social worker, took over.[41] According to Terry, these women were "very good with the children, treating them not only as individuals, but also as human beings."[42] This attitude was very important to Terry and sheds light on why she was so supportive of the hiring of people like Chambers, Dodge, and McDermott. Terry prided herself on being able to relate to a great number of people of all races and social classes largely because of her ability to accept others as they were and her willingness to include—at least when necessary—those whom others might see as unfit companions. Terry likely would have seen this attitude toward children as a first step and requirement in recognizing their importance to society and, in turn, the importance of the juvenile court project as a whole.

The Arkansas legislature called for the establishment of reform schools for juvenile offenders in 1905. Act 199 of that year established the State Reform School to be managed by the State Board of Penitentiary Commissioners and called for the state to "develop [the inmates] morally, intellectually, and industriously, and to teach them some useful trade or avocation." Females were required to be housed separately from males and African Americans separately from whites.[43] The State Reform School did not focus on rehabilitation of the children, however, providing educational lessons only three months out of the year and requiring farm labor for the rest of the time. This was a "place of punishment for bad children."[44] In 1915, the probation officers of Jefferson and Pulaski counties sought the reform and relocation of the State Reform School. This was initially vetoed by Governor Charles Brough, but the Arkansas legislature approved the change in 1917 and reopened the institution as the Boys Industrial School.[45] The only option for female delinquents was the House of the Good Shepherd in Hot Springs and this institution only took "mild cases."[46] Because of this need, the legislature also approved the creation of the Girls Industrial School in 1917.[47] Originally, this new school was set to open in buildings vacated by the State Reform School. In July 1918, however, Martha Falconer came to Little Rock from Washington DC to survey the social situation around Camp Pike. Falconer disliked the site chosen for the new Girls Industrial School and ranked Arkansas forty-sixth in the nation in the care of delinquent girls and women. To rectify the situation, Falconer recommended to the Fosdick Commission the release of $50,000 to be supplemented with matching funds from Arkansas. Mrs. Clio Harper headed up a successful state campaign to raise the necessary funds: $55,000 total.[48] With this new monetary support, a new site was selected for the Girls Industrial School near Alexander, Arkansas.

When the school opened, Blanche Martin, who had been working as a teacher in Little Rock, took charge and set up with the first six girls in a small log house. Early impressions of the school were largely positive due in part to the variety of programs available for the girls: "The setting was spiritually stimulating ... the girls were trained in domestic science, cooking and sewing, as well as in the usual school curriculum ... the girls assisted in farming, gardening, scientific poultry raising and dairying." By 1925, the enrollment had grown to seventy-five girls.[49] Terry, at first pleased with the success of the school, eventually changed her mind about the endeavor. As she explained in her manuscript:

> After a time, however, a man was elected Governor[50] who never should have been, and he regarded the school as one of the places to which he could appoint people who had done him favors and who needed jobs. ... Soon Blanche came to see me and told me that she was going to resign. She said she didn't mind the work, or the low salary, but she couldn't stand the people who were being appointed and who didn't have the same attitudes that she did toward children. I urged her not to resign, saying that the Governor would probably be gone in two years, and if she were to resign she would be entirely out of the picture and would be unable to do anything else with the school. But Blanche, like many other people, did not understand that; instead of staying there, where she could have had some influence on the situation, she resigned.[51]

Shortly after Martin's resignation, Terry realized she did not have anyone available to replace her. Discouraged by the situation, she resigned from the board of the Girls Industrial School.

Although she discontinued her relationship with the Girls Industrial School, Terry continued to work with the Juvenile Court for nineteen years. During her time on the board, she saw the troubles faced by the court as the inadequacies of the laws came into view—

the original law was created as a statute added on to an existing law, causing it to be largely ineffectual. Like Terry, others working with the law were often "seriously hampered and frequently baffled in their attempts to help children to obtain legal care and protection" in Arkansas.[52] Terry continued with the Juvenile Court despite the challenges, however, showing her devotion and willingness to commit herself fully to a project. Her involvement in the establishment of the court system demonstrates the growing boldness of her activism, as well as her vast desire and commitment to help Arkansas youth regardless of the challenges and requirements involved. Because of this work, Terry realized the limitations of the courts firsthand. In a later letter on behalf of a young student jailed for protesting the draft, Terry remarked "you know perfectly well that our courts and our prisons are faulty institutions just as everything else in life is."[53] Remembering her time with the Juvenile Court, Terry remarked:

> I think we have finally come to realize that avoiding trouble is cheaper in the long run than trying to reform people after they had fallen by the wayside and have to be picked up again. In my extreme old age, I am always amused when people try to shield me from knowledge of the sins of the world, because I learned everything about human beings years and years ago. During the nineteen years I was chairman of the juvenile court board I was exposed to everything from robbery to incest, and if I could have been shocked, I would have been shocked long ago.[54]

Selected Photographs

Adolphine Fletcher as an infant; circa 1883. Courtesy of the University of Arkansas at Little Rock Archives, Arkansas Studies Institute.

Adolphine Fletcher, age four; circa 1886. Courtesy of the University of Arkansas at Little Rock Archives, Arkansas Studies Institute.

Colonel John Gould Fletcher Sr. and Adolphine Krause Fletcher (parents of Adolphine Fletcher Terry); undated. Courtesy of the Butler Center for Arkansas Studies, Arkansas Studies Institute.

Adolphine Fletcher, Mary Fletcher, and John Gould Fletcher Jr.; 1894. Courtesy of the Butler Center for Arkansas Studies, Arkansas Studies Institute.

Peabody High School graduating class, Little Rock, Arkansas; 1898.
Adolphine Fletcher is on the right end of the second row from the front.
Courtesy of the Butler Center for Arkansas Studies, Arkansas Studies
Institute.

Vassar College Graduating Class; 1902. Courtesy of the University of
Arkansas at Little Rock Archives, Arkansas Studies Institute.

Adolphine Fletcher as a bridesmaid; undated. Courtesy of the University of Arkansas at Little Rock Archives, Arkansas Studies Institute.

The Pike-Fletcher-Terry House; undated. Constructed in 1840 for Albert Pike and located at 411 East 7th Street in Little Rock, this architectural landmark was listed on the National Register of Historic Places in 1972. Although it has been remodeled several times over the years, especially during its use as Arkansas Female College in the 1870s and afterward when it became a residence again, it retains much of its original Greek Revival style. In 1964, Adolphine Fletcher Terry and her sister Mary Drennan deeded the property to the City of Little Rock, specifying that it be used for the Arkansas Arts Center. The museum located in the house opened as the Decorative Arts Museum in March 1985. In 2004, it became the Arts Center Community Gallery, which exhibits local and regional art. Courtesy of the Butler Center for Arkansas Studies, Arkansas Studies Institute.

Adolphine Fletcher Terry on her wedding day; July 7, 1910. Courtesy of the University of Arkansas at Little Rock Archives, Arkansas Studies Institute.

David Dickson Terry - 1911

David D. Terry; 1911. Courtesy of the University of Arkansas at Little Rock Archives, Arkansas Studies Institute.

Adolphine Fletcher Terry with infant David Terry Jr.; circa 1911. Courtesy of the University of Arkansas at Little Rock Archives, Arkansas Studies Institute.

Pike-Fletcher-Terry House in the 1870s during its time as Arkansas Female College. Lou Krause, Adolphine Krause Fletcher's sister, purchased the house in 1886 and transferred it to John Gould Fletcher Sr. in 1889. The Terrys married in the house in 1910 and spent the rest of their lives there. Courtesy of the Arkansas History Commission.

The Terry family around the dinner table; circa 1930s. Courtesy of the University of Arkansas at Little Rock Archives, Arkansas Studies Institute.

Eleanor Roosevelt and Adolphine Fletcher Terry in New York City during an East Coast tour Terry led in the 1950s for the Arkansas Federation of Women's Clubs. Mrs. Roosevelt lunched with the club women and spoke to them about the United Nations. Courtesy of the University of Arkansas at Little Rock Archives, Arkansas Studies Institute.

WEC members Vivion Brewer, Adolphine Fletcher Terry, and Pat House; November 2, 1963. The WEC disbanded on this date, and Terry was presented with a plaque that read: "In deep appreciation for your unique, selfless and unremitting contribution to humanity and for your inspiration and guidance to the Women's Emergency Committee." Courtesy of the Butler Center for Arkansas Studies, Arkansas Studies Institute.

David D. Terry and Adolphine Fletcher Terry at their 50th wedding anniversary celebration; 1960. Courtesy of the University of Arkansas at Little Rock Archives, Arkansas Studies Institute.

The Terrys with their grandchildren at their 50th wedding anniversary celebration; 1960. Courtesy of the University of Arkansas at Little Rock Archives, Arkansas Studies Institute.

Adolphine Fletcher Terry; circa 1966. Photo originally appeared in the Arkansas Gazette; *copy courtesy of the Butler Center for Arkansas Studies, Arkansas Studies Institute.*

Chapter 4

A Growing Family, World War I, and the Phyllis Wheatley YWCA

In her book *Courage!*, written under the pseudonym Mary Lindsey, Adolphine Fletcher Terry explains how she felt about her life after her work with the Juvenile Court:

> I had always been interested in public affairs, and now had the opportunity to make what I thought was a real contribution to the civic life of our community. There was not a cloud in our horizon; there was not even a mother-in-law in the family who might possibly have been a discordant element ... I planned my life through the years, quite sure of myself, rather impatient with other people, feeling perhaps sorry for and even a little scornful of those who did not have all that I possessed—wonderful health, a pleasant home, and an interesting life. I was not a modest person.[1]

In contrast to her work with school reorganization, Terry walked away from the Juvenile Court project feeling accomplished and ready to become more active in her community. She clearly had a high opinion of herself and the life she had created for her family, and perhaps intended to use her work in the community to perpetuate the image of her seemingly picture-perfect life to those around her. Adding to this happy picture, the Terrys welcomed a baby girl named Mary in 1914. Unlike many women of her class, Terry did not leave her children in the care of a nurse. She had a particular aversion to the African-

American women popular with southern mothers. When remembering the time after the birth of her first child, Terry explained her experiences trying to find a nurse for him and provided some insight into a stereotype associated with African-American women:

> Although young women in the South frequently turned their babies over to cheap negro nurses, I did not. I had learned how frightful the percentage was of those of the race who were afflicted with venereal diseases, especially syphilis. On one occasion I engaged an attractive, well-recommended negro women, but stipulated in advance that she should have a Wassermann test. It was positive. As I could not bring myself to explain to her what the trouble was, I made up an excuse for not taking her, but did not try again. I cared for my own baby, leaving him occasionally to play under the supervision of a young white girl.[2]

After the birth of Mary, however, things became more difficult in the Terry household, as a situation presented itself that shattered Terry's image of her life. According to Terry, "Mary was one of the prettiest babies I have ever seen, or at least I thought she was, and she seemed perfectly normal at first. But Mrs. Herndon, who had nursed me when I had been thrown from the horse, and who had married and retired from nursing but returned to take care of Mary, soon discovered there was something wrong. As a result, we had X-rays taken and they showed that both of her legs had been broken above the knee and had healed before she was born."[3] This discovery showed that Mary had a very serious medical condition, osteogenesis imperfecta, and prompted more than ten years of visiting one specialist after another across the country trying to find a cure or relief. Early in Mary's life, Terry was open to suggestions by friends and doctors, but she often found only contradicting opinions. At one point, she even visited a fortune teller, although she did not expect to find the answers to her troubles. What she did find, however, was a humorous situation that would delight the family for years to come. The appearance of Terry, who often dressed simply and was likely outwardly showing the wear of her current situation, gave the fortune teller the impression that she "lived in another city and was having financial difficulties." The fortune teller went on to describe Terry's "little house, a bungalow, with about seven rooms." She implored Terry to remain strong and "don't give up the bungalow!" Later, when Mary was enjoying a vibrant life, the Terry family adopted this expression as an inside joke.[4]

Her visit to the fortune teller shows how desperate Terry was to find a solution for Mary's painful condition. Mary's illness was a wake-up call for the confident and prideful Terry, who remarked that "the diagnosis of Mary's physical problems had not only been a terrible experience, but also a tremendous blow to my personal pride. Our first child had been so strong and healthy that it never occurred to me that we would have anything but well, normal children. I had been sitting on top of the world, and suddenly my world had been completely shaken."[5]

Terry had formerly viewed the birth of a mentally or physically handicapped child as "the worst grief which could befall a human soul" and believed that in such a case, the mother should put the child out of its misery as an act of mercy.[6] Mary's birth, however, was a turning point in Terry's life. Her experiences with her daughter, especially the reaction of others to Mary and Terry's interactions with other patients in the hospitals, brought her a new understanding of the environment of those pushed aside by the mainstream world. Terry gained a new appreciation for the people she had worked with during her community activism and realized her power to change the lives of others. After encountering a disabled child on a train who was able to see a specialist only after his father's coworkers took up a collection, Terry had a particularly strong reaction to his situation. As she recounts in her autobiography, "I realized that if I had been in his mother's place, I would have lost my mind. If I had to look at my child every day and know we didn't have the money to help him, I would have become an anarchist. ... I could not imagine my own children being unable to have just the ordinary care of a doctor. ... I never forgot the meeting with this child. ... I developed a feeling of gratitude for what I had."[7]

From these experiences with Mary, she learned to actively live life with little thought as to what others expected of her—"however difficult, I have always preferred to meet a circumstance actively, rather than passively wait for something, whether good or bad, to transpire."[8] Later, she would face many obstacles while trying to allow Mary to live a normal and happy life, but she would not back down from these challenges or from an opportunity to help her community. Before she could take on any additional projects, however, Terry welcomed her third child, Sally, in 1916.

Soon after the birth of Sally Terry, the United States entered World War I with a congressional declaration on April 6, 1917. This was a particularly tough situation for Terry, a pacifist of German descent who remained largely naïve about the complexities of world relations. Terry saw the United States' entrance as a "devastating blow." Terry believed that war had been eliminated "with all the interchanges among the nations of the world, the telephones, telegraphs, trade and commerce. And when, in the midst of my personal grief over Mary's affliction, the war broke out, I thought I had lost my mind."[9] Terry elaborated on her view of the situation: "Murder had suddenly become not only respectable, but heroic and glamorous. I walked around as if I were in a complete daze. I felt as if my world had washed away and I had nothing to stand on, and I realized that I needed more to believe in."[10] Her reaction may be considered a little overly dramatic by some, but her compassion for the individuals affected by war is undeniable.

Terry turned to religion to help her through this difficult time. Although Terry attended church throughout her life, she "thought that religion made very little difference. I was not an atheist; I was not anything. ... Religion was not a serious thing to me."[11] Terry's beliefs about religion were very open; she believed that it was more important to believe in God than worry about what he was called. She explained,

"The Jews fundamentally followed the teachings of Moses, who I think must have been the greatest man who ever lived. I'll leave out Jesus, for it seems to me he was more than human, although what he was, I don't know, and I'd rather leave it like that. I'm not really sure that any of the great religious leaders were or are completely human, and I don't think it makes a particle of difference."[12] Terry was a member of the Episcopal Church and taught Sunday School for ten years.[13] This time during World War I was one of the first times in which she turned to her religious beliefs for support and strength.

David D. Terry Sr. enlisted in the U.S. Army on June 5, 1918, and was stationed at Camp Pike, leaving Adolphine to run the household.[14] Here, she faced the distressing situation of being of German descent in a very anti-German environment. The propaganda of the time spread the distrust of and animosity toward Germans and even German goods. In April 1918, the Little Rock School District suspended the teaching of the German language to its students, and other schools in Arkansas followed suit.[15] In addition to a backlash against all things German, many Germans experienced episodes of violence, especially if they were seen to be unwilling to do the "proper" patriotic activities. Terry's standing in the community protected her from any violent attacks, but she was still the subject of a number of rumors. For example, when David Terry enlisted in the army, many of their neighbors decided that Adolphine was "so pro-German that Dave couldn't take it anymore" and had joined the army to escape from her while making plans for a future divorce. Imagine their surprise when the couple showed up together for dinner at the local country club: "When we came in side by side, me with my corsage, people looked perfectly aghast, and I wondered what was so strange about us."[16] Terry commented on her life in Little Rock during this time:

> There were various types of war work to be done, but if people did-
> n't knit or serve in the Red Cross, they could always hunt spies or
> carry tales about their neighbors who had German ancestors. It was

really a dreadful time. People were suspicious of anyone who even had a German name. My cousins, the Hotzes, whose original ancestor had left Germany about 1830, were under suspicion even though Clara was running the work room for the Red Cross and was engaged to an Army officer. They had all been born in this country and had never thought of being anything other than loyal citizens, but nevertheless they were under suspicion by their neighbors.[17]

In addition to her first-hand experience with the hostility and her perception of the discrimination against the Hotzes, Terry saw another instance of the anti-German feeling through the experiences of a young German girl named Freda. Freda had been visiting a German professor at an eastern university when World War I broke out and was advised by her family to remain in the United States until the war ended. She ended up in Little Rock, making her living selling the Harper Method of hair care and styling. At first, the Little Rock community welcomed Freda, but its opinion soon soured and she could no longer earn enough money to support herself.[18] Terry explained Freda's experiences in her manuscript, "Freda was asked to attend a dance at one of the large hotels, and when the officer's wife saw Freda there it set her off. She was sure that Freda was a spy and was here to collect information. She spread that rumor and within a week Freda didn't have a single client. Freda couldn't return to her original hosts in the east … she really had no place to go."[19] Always willing to help someone in need, Terry took in Freda, who had been tutoring David Jr. According to Terry, "I wasn't one of the idiots who thought it was time to do away with the German language, so I suggested that she move in with us and continue the lessons to earn her room and board."[20] In contrast to Freda's situation, however, World War I created new opportunities for women nationally. Women were encouraged to start victory gardens and use their clubs to raise money and gather supplies for the American soldiers. Women in locations where a large number of men were drafted were able to break into the workforce with new jobs and more important roles.

Nationally, women had continued to fight for suffrage leading up to and during World War I, as they had since 1848. The southern suffrage movement, however, which was often hindered by the restrictive image of southern womanhood, did not take firm hold until the 1890s, before declining and rebounding during a second wave during the 1910s.[21] This second movement would prove to be more effective than the first in the South, with more women willing to join the movement. In the interim between the two waves, "southern women had gained the necessary experiences that tended to galvanize suffrage sentiment. The forces that had long restrained women's activism … had given way."[22]

In Arkansas, the movement for suffrage was typical of many southern states. Arkansas suffrage groups started during the 1880s with the first group formed in Eureka Springs in 1885 and later the Equal Suffrage League formed in Little Rock in 1888. In actuality, the issue first appeared during the 1868 constitutional convention—raised by a man—and was predictably met with much ridicule.[23] The Equal Suffrage League existed for only five years, but during this time, its members published a journal called the *Woman's Chronicle*. This journal was printed weekly and, in addition to its regular subscribers, was distributed to members of the legislature when in session.[24]

The Equal Suffrage League eventually fizzled out and was not replaced until 1911 when the Political Equality League of Little Rock was created with Mary Fletcher, sister of Adolphine Terry, as president. This group had mainly middle-class members—including eight men as original members—and, according to historian Carl Moneyhon, was the beginning of a statewide suffrage movement in Arkansas. The league met twice a month and sponsored educational programs. Although active, the group was ultimately unable to convince the Arkansas legislature to pass any bills.[25] According to Terry, Mary had been elected because she did not have a husband who could object to her participation. The Terry sisters were described as "very active workers for Suffrage during the first years of the organization. Indeed it was not until the work was well under way that they relaxed their efforts."[26] In her autobiography, however, Terry only refers to marching in the downtown parade without any objection from her husband. The first year the amendment came before the Arkansas legislature, the league "picked out the pretty girls to sit in the gallery," and those chosen had to deal with abuse from the legislators.[27] Terry participated with the Political Equality League (later the Arkansas Women's Suffrage Association and Equal Suffrage State Central Committee) as it approached the Arkansas legislature in 1911, 1913, 1915, and 1917, when women won the right to vote in primary elections.[28] Arkansas women voted in their first primary election in May 1918.[29] Eventually, the U.S. Congress approved the Nineteenth Amendment, giving suffrage to women. After a whirlwind of campaigning by Arkansas women, the Arkansas legislature voted to ratify the Amendment on July 28, 1919, becoming the twelfth state of the Union and only the second of the southern states to do so. The Nineteenth Amendment officially became part of the U.S. Constitution in 1920, finally granting women equal voting rights.[30]

Reflecting on this movement in a 1969 *Arkansas Gazette* article, Terry stated, "We acted like complete hellions to get the vote. We of the 'lady' class had always been on a pedestal ... beauteous womanhood, all that kind of junk. The men had looked up to us, idolized us. They had changed their attitude when we tied ourselves to telephone poles and did the most unseemly and unladylike things to attract attention to our cause. The Negroes and the college students are using the same tactics today. It's funny, but you just have to do it. 'Ladies' and 'Uncle Tom's' don't get anywhere." Later, Terry served as an original member of the League of Women Voters in Pulaski County.[31] She always cherished her right to vote: "To me, the vote represents more than just saying how a person feels about an issue of a candidate, it represents human dignity and the fact that a citizen can express his or her opinion on any subject without fear of reprisal. That, I think, is what real human dignity consists of."[32]

In addition to her work with the suffrage movement, Terry took on another project soon after the end of World War I and served on an advisory committee for a group of women establishing an African-American branch of the Young Women's Christian Association (YWCA) in Little Rock. The campaign for the branch started in March 1918 and quickly garnered the support of many in the local African-American community. According to historian Peggy Harris, the YWCA was "interested in serving, in particular, those women and girls who lived near military camps" at the request of the U.S. War Department Commission on Training Activities and the YMCA. Little Rock—because of its proximity to Camp Pike, Fort Roots, and Eberts Field—was a "prime location."[33] By March 1919, the national YWCA Committee on Colored Work started the process of construction of an African-American branch in Little Rock with a $40,000 budget.[34]

This project had great significance for Terry; much like the juvenile court project in which she was willing to go against community expectations to help Arkansas children, this project saw Terry openly supporting an African-American organization, an undesirable venture for many white women in Little Rock. White women who worked with black organizations and for black causes often "recapitulated women's historic social housekeeping role. They concentrated their efforts on nurturing grassroots leadership, building networks of sympathetic volunteers across racial lines, and providing ways for genuine cross-racial friendships to develop. Their vision reached beyond the establishment of equal opportunity; they sought ways for individuals across race and class divides to genuinely appreciate and support one another."[35] Terry saw her work with the YWCA as a way to help local African-American women establish an institution equal to that available to whites and in the process she learned that the women were intelligent and capable of reaching their goal. She agreed to this project largely because she did not believe any other white women, especially of her social standing, would be willing to attach their name to the project and she felt an obligation to step in where they would not. During this experience, Terry learned to look at her African-American counterparts in a new light. While she had believed in equality for all people for many years, Terry now realized that she could cultivate relationships with these African-American women outside of her usual charitable activities.

According to a 1945 article by Dorothy I. Height, the YWCA "made special effort to reach different groups of girls and women including members of racial minority groups. They [association organizers] were sincere in their efforts to make the Association a true cross section of women and girls of different economic, social, racial and religious background to achieve a better life for all."[36] In Little Rock, the existing YWCA would not allow the new African-American group to use the official name. Instead, the branch became known as the Phyllis Wheatley Club.[37] Although most white YWCA organizations in the South were not welcoming to their black counterparts, the YWCA on a national level had long accepted African-American women, particularly young girls, as a part of the club. According to a 1940 article, amongst the YWCA members:

> There has been the idea of togetherness in all that was done. Partly because of the fact that some work was already organized for Negroes by Negroes under the name of the Y.W.C.A.; partly because of the belief of the Association in neutral groupings—occupational, racial, nationality; and, particularly in the early years of the Association, partly because of the uncritical following of existing American folkways, there does today exist in the Y.W.C.A. a great deal of work with Negroes in separate units—branches, and Negro clubs.[38]

By 1940, for example, the YWCA had seventy-six recorded African-American units and 186 white units with African-American specific groups and activities.[39] By 1945, the number of African-American

84

units increased to eighty-three and, outside of the southern states, new units did not form separate branches.[40] It is important to note, however, that the association did not officially endorse desegregation of branches until 1946.[41]

The National YWCA Public Affairs Committee identified four "areas of concern" regarding African-American girls at the end of the 1930s. These areas included "inter-racial cooperation rather than separation … economic opportunities for Negroes … the support of Negroes in the exercise of their basic civil rights, and support of anti-lynching legislation."[42] Terry joined an advisory board for the club, but was surprised to find out that she was not needed. As she explained:

> The women who served as directors of the club were all well educated and leaders of their community, and they had plenty of ideas of their own. We, the advisers, got more out of the experience than we gave, because we made friends among these black women who since the Civil War had never been thought of as possible friends of ours, and who had lived in a world apart. They were the wives of professional men, and they provided us with an education. We, the daughters of Confederate veterans who had heard a great deal about the white side of the war, now learned of the suffering of the black population, before, during and after the war, and of the lacks from which they still suffered.[43]

This was a common experience for those serving on YWCA boards and committees, both black and white. Height argues that "one of the strongest assets of the YWCA is the experience it gives in policy making to women serving on its boards, councils and committees. Such experience contributes to the development of woman's sense of citizenship responsibility and in the skills needed to carry that responsibility. [Branches] are increasingly moving more and more to the participation of Negro and white women together on boards and committees."[44] Terry remembered the African-American women from the project as a "fine, well educated, intelligent group: teachers, school principals, wives of professional men, who worked untiringly for the advancement of the race to which they belonged although actually some were more white than colored. ... They wanted equality of opportunity for their race and they wanted to be treated as human, not subhuman beings."[45] Although her work with the group was limited, Terry's involvement with the YWCA represents her willingness to step out of her social comfort zone and participate in the project even when "the members of the board of directors of the white YWCA wouldn't touch the whole project with a forty foot pole."[46]

In Little Rock, the Phyllis Wheatley YWCA opened to the public in 1921 as "the established group for YW work among black women and girls ... and the only recreational facility for blacks."[47] Immediately, the branch was successful. According to Harris, in its first year of operation in the new building, it organized "thirty-five Girl Reserve Clubs, five recreational clubs and thirty-two vesper services" and was visited by 3,318 people.[48] Little Rock's Phyllis Wheatley YWCA closed in 1971 when it was absorbed by the Central YWCA.[49]

Soon after its founding, the Phyllis Wheatley YWCA became an original member of the Community Chest, a forerunner of the United Way and another of Terry's projects. The support from the Community Chest allowed the Phyllis Wheatley YWCA to better serve the black community.[50]

Chapter 5

Congressional Campaigning, Americanism, and Arkansas Libraries

A s Adolphine Terry worked with the YWCA, the world moved into the 1920s. The image that comes to mind when one thinks about American women in the 1920s is generally that of the classic flapper: a single girl—a smoker with bobbed hair and a boyish figure. The flapper had exposed legs and tweezed eyebrows. She wore makeup and risqué clothing with low waists, low necks, and no corset.[1] This is the image that represents the "roaring twenties" to today's generations, standing for everything viewed as important from that decade of revolution and experimentation during the time between World War I and the Depression. Like the stylish Gibson girl for the 1890s, the image of the flapper for the 1920s "epitomized the then prevailing conceptions of woman and her role."[2] This image is not representative of Terry during the 1920s, however. Unlike her flapper counterparts, Terry, a middle-aged mother, did not use the expanding freedom for women as an excuse to tighten her dresses or tweeze her eyebrows—those types of issues did not concern Terry, who dressed plainly and practically most days. Instead, she took this opportunity to immerse herself deeper into local politics. In contrast to the popular image of the flapper, Terry is representative of other women of her age, class, and economic standing.

American women had won the right to vote and entered the 1920s optimistic about their political participation and their new role in the home and workplace. For many women, the right to vote was more than a political opportunity, it was "a symbol of something much larger—the image of the new woman."[3] Feminism in the '20s has been interpreted very differently by historians over the years. American women stepped into their new political and economic roles, but they continued to work for the rights of women and children, an arena in which their actions were generally safe and tolerated. While women tended not to differ from their male counterparts in the way that they voted, it is important to note that "those states which had lived longest under equal suffrage were usually very advanced in welfare legislation, and especially laws to protect the right of women and children."[4] It had been a common hope of the time that women would vote together as a large group, causing a wave of significant changes in American politics. In reality, however, votes were cast by women for as many varied reasons as they were cast by men. Historian Anne Firor Scott argues that "the South had adopted a more rigid definition of the role of women ... and had elevated that definition to the position of a myth."[5] Scott explains that southern women "were supposed to be beautiful, gentle, efficient, morally superior, and, at the same time, ready to accept the doctrine of male superiority and authority."[6] She cites a large move into politics by southern women (particularly for labor and child protection laws) but contends that most sought to uphold their ladylike image and expected feminine qualities.[7] This is especially true for Terry, who tried to maintain the "proper" image throughout her husband's political campaign and time in Congress, even to the point of annoyance and exhaustion on her part. Although Terry had shown herself willing to step outside of these cultural conventions in some of her past projects, she was well aware of the repercussions to her husband's campaign if she did not maintain the expected image of her family.

Adolphine Terry was certainly not a typical flapper girl; instead she represented the image of the majority of married women in Arkansas at that time—concerned about family and home. Particularly worried about the lack of healthy children to carry on the family name, Terry explained, "Dave and I really liked children and we both enjoyed them, as well as liked them as people. I felt apologetic to him, though, for not being able to give him a family of strong husky children."[8] It was during this time that the Terry family grew once again with the birth of William (Bill) Terry on October 11, 1922.[9] Adolphine Terry later remarked on her happiness at the birth of a healthy child: "[My happy college life] doesn't compare with the way I felt as your wife and as the mother of David and Billy." David D. Terry spent a great deal of time away from the family during the 1920s while trying to catch up on the work suspended during his service in World War I. In a letter written to Adolphine in 1922, David D. Terry remarked, "It is not necessary for you to classify and enumerate the attraction of the children to make me want to go see them. I have missed the whole bunch of you terrible [sic] and nothing would suit me better than to drop everything, mortgage my few possessions, and catch the next train north."[10] As mentioned in the letter, the family continued its routine of spending many summers in the cooler climate of the north due to Mary's health.[11] During one of these vacations, Terry took Mary to visit a doctor in Boston, Massachusetts. She relates:

> Mary was in the hospital a month having all sorts of tests. She had a good time because all the nurses were kind to her, and since she was not ill she could come and go as she wanted to. The biggest attraction there was a small child, an orphan who was not quite a year old. Mary became infatuated with him, and he fell completely in love with her. She took me around to see him one day and when she picked him up, he snuggled back in her arms and seemed perfectly at home.[12]

Mary was not the only one attached to the little boy named Joe. Terry herself soon decided to adopt the child, seeing this as a perfect opportunity to fulfill one of her plans for Mary and as a way to help a child in need. Terry explained her plan to adopt a child for Mary later in life when others Mary's age were starting families. She realized that Mary "was still a little young for this, but here was this child who needed a home and in whom Mary was very much interested."[13] Adolphine corresponded with David about the possible adoption, and he first suggested caution: "I know a little homeless child is about the most appealing thing in the world, but you should consider the matter from all sides before you rush to follow the dictates of an unusually compassionate heart"[14]—then warmed up to the idea—"You may be the instrument through which it is given him to grow into a useful citizen."[15] Terry's "unusually compassionate heart" won out, and Joe became the fifth child in the Terry family, much to the surprise of David D. Terry: "I thought I had written ahead to Dave and explained, very tactfully, that I was bringing home a baby. But either he misunderstood or I didn't explain as well as I thought I had, for when I got off of the train with Joe on my arm, I could tell that he was completely bowled over, although he never said a word. He was accustomed to the kind of life we had, and I think he liked it; he certainly was never bored."[16] Much like her work with the juvenile court, Terry's adoption of Joe shows her strong commitment to helping others. Terry brought Joe into her home, willing to do what it took to raise the child as one of her own when she could have considered him another project to spend a little time with and then walk away.

While the demands of her large family lessened the time Terry could spend on extensive outside activism, she soon found herself with another project requiring her attention—the political career of David D. Terry, who served in the Arkansas House of Representatives in 1933 followed by the U.S. House of Representatives from January 3, 1934, to January 2, 1943. During each campaign, Adolphine helped to schedule the family activities—determining who would be at each political rally, dinner, or speech; who would drive the family to each location; who would speak to the crowd—as well as coordinated with the campaign staff. Terry committed herself fully to her husband's campaign, attending a number of uncomfortable events to help with the family image and "[making] as many friends as possible for the Terrys."[17]

David D. Terry's father, William Leake Terry, served in the Arkansas legislature in 1879 and 1881 and in the U.S. House of Representatives from 1891 to 1901. After the resignation of Heartsill Ragon from the Arkansas legislature, David Terry followed in his father's footsteps and entered the race. The Terry family quickly started to campaign in preparation for a special election held in December of 1933. During this first campaign, David Terry's fiercest opponent was Brooks Hays (U.S. House of Representatives 1943–1959). In a diary kept during the campaign, Terry accuses Hays of "letting his workers spread rumors that David and Adolphine Terry were cousins and their children 'all degenerates.'" Other opponents accused the Terrys of being "black with money, too snooty to speak to the ordinary person." While on a speaking tour, Adolphine Terry sought to fight this image of the family by wearing "dollar dresses and a meek black hat that had been rained on." In addition, she dressed the children in overalls and let them run around barefoot.[18] Always strong in the face of criticism and challenges, Terry did not let this kind of campaigning affect her. In fact, Terry remained more concerned with how her actions might reflect negatively on the campaign. For example, she gave $5 to Mabel Braughman to run for the Arkansas Senate—it was rare for Terry to turn away those looking for help, monetary or otherwise, especially if they had a particular cause in mind—and was very concerned that it might lose some support for Dave.[19]

Terry approached her husband's political campaign with the same commitment and temperament as she did her other projects. She explained her thoughts about the campaign in her autobiography:

Every community that wanted to raise money had a rally and invited all the candidates. ... It wasn't necessary to spend much money, but this was during the depression and people were counting everything they spent. Some of the candidates really couldn't afford even a limited kind of campaign, but politics is a strange thing. ... We never bought any votes and we never saw anyone else doing that, but we tried to get people on our side by spending money in our campaign. For instance, at the rally dinners, which were generally sponsored by the local Parent Teacher Association, there was usually food left over. When the rally was finished, I would go around back and meet the women who had done the cooking and buy some of the leftovers to bring home with me.[20]

Terry was committed to campaigning for her husband, whether it was buying leftovers from people who desperately needed the money, passing out flyers, or speaking with anyone who would listen. As a wealthy woman dealing with a struggling public, she used her talents as a speaker to help her through this time. According to Terry, she was "the world's best listener, for I do think that a sympathetic listener is a thing a great many people need." She explains that many of her listeners had "certainty fallen victim, not to my charms, but to my ability to let people talk about themselves."[21]

After success in the Arkansas legislature, David Terry moved on to national government. He served as a Democrat in the U.S. House of Representatives from 1934 to 1943 but left Congress after an unsuccessful bid for a seat in the Senate in 1942. While in office, he continued the Terry family commitment to education by sponsoring an education funding bill. This bill, signed by President Roosevelt in 1935, marked the first time federal assistance was authorized for public school districts.[22] Adolphine's commitment did not end with her husband's election, however. She became very active in the Arkansas Women's Democratic Club and was elected as vice chairman of the Arkansas Democratic State Central Committee in 1940. She also served as a speaker for the Women's Committee of the Democratic National Committee, traveling across the country talking about women and politics.[23] Although she often joined David in Washington DC, as was typical of many congressional wives, Terry spent most of her time in Little Rock so she could be close to the family and keep an eye on the local political scene. The Great Depression had struck Arkansas, leaving a large number of people in need of help. In February of 1931, for example, the Red Cross distributed food allowances to 519,000 Arkansans.[24] This number likely does not represent the full number eligible for or in need of such allowances, since many residents were reluctant to take the aid offered by Red Cross workers.[25] Terry received a number of letters while in Arkansas and in Washington DC asking for boxes of clothing for families, often rural, in exchange for preserves or fruit. These letters were often written on whatever scraps of paper were handy and were sometimes dictated to a neighbor or friend by an illiterate person.[26] Terry kept a box of donated and old clothes in her home, and she only occasionally accepted what the families in need offered to her.

While David D. Terry ran for and served in Congress, Adolphine Terry found herself filling her new role as a politician's wife. The change was not always easy for Terry. She explained the delicate balance between standing for her own seemingly liberal beliefs while still keeping to the middle of the road during the campaign: "Many times in my life I have felt as if I were teetering on the brink of a volcano."[27] In her autobiography, Terry describes a typical campaign week in July 1934: "On July second of that year, we were to have a meeting to plan the serving of lunches and dinners on election day to the clerks and judges of the second ward ... it was the sort of thing I disliked to do."[28] Later in the afternoon, the family headed to Perryville to deliver books to the new library. They arrived home at midnight after a dinner and dance for the library dedication. The next day was spent scheduling for July 4th activities. Terry had the help of her son, David, and had to wait two hours in the campaign office to secure a meeting with her husband and his campaign manager, Gilroy Cox. The rest of the week was filled with rushed visits, sweltering hot events, and speech writing.[29]

In addition to her campaigning activities, Terry was anonymously volunteered to give a speech on "The Need of Women's Interest in the Planning Movement" at a July 1934 dinner of the Arkansas State Planning Progress Committee. Although she only "had a general idea of what the planning movement was" and "didn't see how or why women's interests could be separated from men's," Terry was excited by the opportunity to deliver the speech, largely because she was speaking with important political figures like the governor and senator Joe T. Robinson. She had been unaware of this engagement and did not know exactly what to speak about during her scheduled time, but her ability to speak to a group pulled her through this situation successfully.[30]

Alongside the strenuous campaigning and official appearances, all while caring for her family, Terry committed herself to a number of organizations and projects. Some of these she willingly took part in, while others she reluctantly joined because it was expected of her. In one particular case, she joined a project as an obligation, committed herself fully, and was pleased with the outcome. According to the entries in her diary for July 28, 1934, the nominating committee of the American Legion Auxiliary approached Terry twice about accepting the position of chairman of the Committee of Americanism, but she refused. The third time the committee asked, however, David D. Terry had opposition in his political race and she took the offer more seriously. She explained: "It is the last thing on earth that I want to do, and I pointed out [to my husband] it would mean my staying in Little Rock all next winter, but after thoroughly canvassing the situation we decided that I should accept the position, and [my husband] would recognize it as a complete and perfect sacrifice on my part to his political career."[31]

She took pleasure in the thought that she "would be repaid if I heard that the wife of one of Dave's opponents bit herself when she read the news in the morning paper and gave herself hydrophobia."[32]

Adolphine Terry also joined the Democratic Club during this time because she "thought David, Jr. might go into politics some day, and it might react against him if I had declined to be a member."[33] Terry later remarked in her diary, "I accepted a membership in this [Distinguished Guest Committee of the Women's City Club] because I'm accepting everything these days."[34]

Despite her membership in a large number of women's clubs, Terry did not always hold her colleagues in the highest opinion and often resented their preoccupation with the social, rather than service, side of the organization. She stated, "These women's organizations are strange things—clothes seem to be the main consideration."[35] Terry was well aware of the role she needed to fill as a political wife and was willing to make whatever sacrifices were necessary.

Terry's work with Arkansas public libraries is perhaps her best-known activity next to her role with the Women's Emergency Committee to Open Our Schools during the Central High desegregation crisis. The library project came to Terry because of her work with the Committee of Americanism of the American Legion Auxiliary. The purpose of the Americanism committee of the Auxiliary today is "to inspire, recognize, and perpetuate responsible citizenship through education and acts of patriotism, in order to raise awareness and increase appreciation of the price paid for our fundamental freedoms."[36] In Terry's time, the committee strived to promote community involvement and advancement. The term "Americanism," which could seem to promote blind patriotism, might have been unappealing to Terry considering the hostile environment she experienced during World War I. According to Terry:

> The word [Americanism] was not popular with me and I had no idea what would be involved, but I accepted and went to my first meeting with many misgivings. I opened the pamphlet which was given to me and found that our first and chief duty was to get books into the hands of our young people; in other words, to establish libraries. That was the thing I most wanted to do. Reading is only a

tool; to teach children to read and not give them something worth-while to read is a waste of time and money.[37]

Echoing these sentiments, in a diary kept during 1934, Terry remarked, "I casually accepted a position last summer as chairman of the Americanism Committee of the local Auxiliary—again the wife of a politician, for I had never been to a meeting of the organization—and found that the committee had been asked by the national to put on a library program. Nothing could have pleased me more. ... I did-n't do this library work for political reasons, but it is awfully good pol-itics, just the same."[38]

The Americanism committee became devoted to Arkansas libraries after the state was accused of being "the most bookless state in the union" at a national Auxiliary meeting. According to Terry, when she joined the project, Arkansas had "three feebly functioning public libraries" after the loss of others during the Depression.[39] The first library in Arkansas was likely established by William E. Woodruff. His Little Rock Circulation Library opened in 1843, allowing visitors to check out books for a $2 annual fee. During the Union occupation of Little Rock during the Civil War, books from the Woodruff library were stored in a home. When a nearby building caught fire, the books were removed onto the street and many of the passing soldiers took the books. A 1901 law allowed for the establishment of public libraries by select cities but provided no means of funding the projects. Tax funds were authorized for libraries by the Arkansas legislature in 1903, and the Arkansas Library Association was organized through the sup-port of the Arkansas Federation of Women's Clubs (AFWC) in 1911. Many of the subscription and fee libraries established in the late nine-teenth and early twentieth century used the new tax funds to become free public libraries. For example, the Helena library, established in 1889, was the first Arkansas library to receive tax funds under a new law of 1911 and became a free institution in 1919. A major develop-ment in Arkansas libraries came in 1921 with the establishment of the

Arkansas Free Library Service Bureau after the AFWC petitioned the legislature and collected books to send out to Arkansas counties that did not have libraries. The legislature established the public library system in connection with the State Department of Education but did not set aside funding for the program until 1923 when it allowed a small fund for traveling libraries. This lack of government support led to the closing of multiple libraries, the discontinuation of the state free-library system, and the loss of the state librarian position as the Depression reached Arkansas. According to sources at the time, 1,600,000 people out of Arkansas's population of 1,800,000 were without regular access to library services. Many women's groups, including the American Legion Auxiliary, campaigned for library support and organization.[40]

For this particular project, Bess Proctor, president of the Arkansas Auxiliary, called on Terry to head a separate library committee. The committee secured Federal Emergency Relief Administration (FERA) funds to reestablish the free-library system in towns with populations greater than 5,000 and for the reinstatement of the state librarian, Christine Sanders.[41] With funding secured, the biggest need of the project was books. To get the Auxiliary started, Terry approached the heirs of a number of local deceased community men. Through this tactic, she secured a large number of books the families did not have space for, including large collections from the families of Judge McCain, George Peay, and P. C. Dooley.[42] Terry then approached the local American Legion groups inquiring about housing for the books. The Legion was building small "huts" to serve as community social centers in many towns across Arkansas. Terry's committee offered the communities 200 books and advice on starting libraries to serve in these community centers. Vincent Mills, the Legion commander, accepted Terry's proposal and went one step further by building small rooms onto many of the huts to serve as public libraries. Terry described the outstanding local response: "The whole thing was a glorious success. We had expected six

97

or eight units to accept, but over a hundred did. The books were brought to our house and sorted. We packed them in boxes provided by a local grocery store and most of them were delivered by David in his old Ford."[43] In areas where Legion huts were not available, the Auxiliary sought out appropriate housing in area businesses and public areas, often helping to locate furnishings for the libraries. Local Auxiliary units and other women's groups cared for the libraries after their initial establishment. From June to August of 1934, six free libraries were established across Arkansas and eight more were being planned under Terry's guidance as "chairman of the Americanism Committee and [in] charge of the library projects for the state department of the Auxiliary in cooperation with FERA."[44] Terry and the Auxiliary continued to help communities start public libraries until their funding ran out.

In addition to hands-on work in the communities, Terry's committee worked to regain governmental support for Arkansas libraries. To this end, the women worked to have a bill introduced to set up an official library program recommended by the American Library Association. Act 177 of 1931, "An Act For the Government of Public Libraries," established that municipal authorities could establish and run local libraries or reading rooms with financial support of a "minimum appropriation of one-half mill from the revenue derived from all real and personal property within the city limits to be used exclusively for the maintenance of such library or reading room." The Arkansas legislature approved funding for the library program in 1935.[45] Recognizing the important work of the Auxiliary, Governor Junius Futrell appointed Bess Proctor to the first Library Commission in Arkansas.[46] The project was well-received and remembered by the small communities the Auxiliary helped. Terry recalled praise she received in a letter on her ninety-first birthday:

> I well remember the hot day in August that my husband and I came to your home to pick up the first books that you had collected from your many friends, and yourself, for our library. Perry County and

Perryville have been the recipients of your service, during the Depression, in starting our first library. No one else had ever thought of doing such a service, just did not think it could be done, and you did it by Faith. Our library has grown into a very nice thing. ... For years I had to appear before the Quorum Court and ask for help ... Now, the Court makes our allowances without all of this begging.[47]

Adolphine Fletcher Terry served as a trustee of the Little Rock Public Library until her retirement in 1966. A branch of the Central Arkansas Library System is named in her honor.

Chapter 6

Compassionate Humanitarianism and Urban Development

While her work with Arkansas libraries and the Juvenile Court remained ongoing and David D. Terry continued to campaign for and serve in Congress, Terry still found time to work on a number of other projects and to help those who asked for her assistance. By this time, Little Rock viewed Terry as someone always willing to help those around her and treated her as such:

> While I remained in Little Rock, I was involved in a number of projects, and practically kept office hours. Because I had lived here all my life, many people know me or had heard of me; when they had tried writing to various officials with no result, they would come to me and I would see what I could do to help. For many years I had been in the habit of taking up any good works which came to the front door, and I have reached a point where I was pretty successful.[1]

Terry often took individuals into her care and went to extraordinary lengths to influence their lives. For example, Terry related in her manuscript the stories of a number of young men and families she attempted to help and described her methods for coping with the growing call for her assistance: "During the years when there had been only one or two callers a week, I was glad to listen and never found it a burden. But the depression had brought so many that I finally emulated Mrs. Roosevelt and took up knitting again. It helped. However sympathetic, I had become too nervous to sit and listen intelligently to other people's worries and offer sensible advice unless I could do something with my hands."[2] One woman, for example, was struggling to support her family after the unexpected death of her husband. She sought help from Terry for her son Robert Wood—"I've tried to see the Governor, but couldn't get in. ... A friend told me that you might be able to help."[3] It speaks to Terry's position in Little Rock that this woman saw her as an acceptable alternative to the governor. Terry immediately immersed herself in Robert's situation and tried to help the family. Robert had spent time in jail for forging a check and was again in jail because he owed money to his employer. Terry tried to help the mother contact relatives who could lend Robert the money he needed. When this did not pan out, Terry helped the woman get a loan from the bank. Terry commented on Robert's situation in her manuscript:

> It was apparent that Robert was not very promising material. His experiences at the state prison farm must have hurt his pride and self-respect, but he came from decent, hard-working parents and had done well during his youth. There is such a thin line between success and failure and because of it, some individuals have great difficulty arriving at maturity. ... Money or material possessions can be replaced, but a character which has been destroyed cannot be. A hundred and sixty-five dollars, I decided, seemed a very small sum in terms of a human soul.[4]

With Terry's help, Robert was released from jail, but the kindness did not have an effect on him and Terry soon got word that he was back in police custody. Still committed to helping the young man, Terry spoke with the executive secretary of the County Welfare Commission and called together of group of "distinguished citizens" including the executive secretaries of the YMCA, the Family Service Agency, and the Boys' Club; the president of the Ministerial Alliance; and the superintendent of schools. By the end of the meeting, the group had Robert sent to the state hospital for observation, effectively getting him out of jail and buying some time to find a permanent solution. Eventually, they got Robert a place in a Youth Administration Camp and he later joined the army.[5] Terry, who had known Robert for only a short time, went to great lengths to help him, involving multiple county and city agencies in his life. It is hard to imagine very many people doing so much to help a stranger, but it was a normal situation for Terry.

Terry provides another example in her manuscript—that of a young man named William with a difficult family life. Terry first met him when he came to her home looking for work, and she gave William and his family $50 to accompany an older brother to California to start a new life. Although she knew "we were doing the wrong thing," she gave the family the benefit of the doubt and tried to help. Within six months, the family returned to Arkansas.[6] Terry tried to help William a number of other times, but eventually had to stop. As she recalled in her manuscript, William returned to Arkansas to secure a divorce so he could marry his new girlfriend, and Terry helped as much as she could with the arrangements. As she related, however, later:

> William showed up with a rather pretty girl whom he introduced as his wife. He said that when he saw her again he realized that she was the one he loved, and he wanted me to give them the money so they could both go to California. I wished them well, but I drew the line and did not give him the money. I had realized by then that it is generally useless to try to bring a person up, or reform him in any way, without changing the whole family, and we had been unable to do that. I was not successful with William.[7]

Robert and William are only two of the large number of individuals whom Terry took a personal interest in. In addition to working with the needy who came to her door looking for work or for guidance, Terry worked with (and in many cases helped to organize) a number of projects in Arkansas, including the Pulaski County Tuberculosis Association and the Community Chest, as well as served as a board member for a number of local organizations.[8]

These types of projects and commitments kept Terry occupied as her children grew and left home. Terry also continued her duties as the wife of a congressman and soon found herself trying to cope with America's entrance into World War II. Terry described this time as "the most terrible days [man] has ever lived through" with events that "seemed fantastic in their horror."[9] During the build-up to and the aftermath of the American entrance into the war, Terry worked closely with a number of Democratic clubs. For example, she served as one of the six "Chairmen of Ushers" at the National Institute of Government sponsored by the Women's Democratic National Committee in 1940 and gave a speech titled "Women and National Defense" in Fayetteville, Arkansas, as vice chairman of the Arkansas Democratic Committee in 1941.[10] Following the events of the war closely and expecting an American entrance at any moment, Terry was not surprised when the Japanese forces attacked, but this does not mean she was any less affected by the event:

> On December seventh, the hour struck; and, like all the other democracies, the U.S. seemed to have been caught in bed. That afternoon I had gone to North Little Rock to say a few words at the dedication of a new housing project, and the mayor brought us the news. ... I sat there, looking up into the clear, cold blue sky of Arkansas, and thought of all the people dying at Pearl Harbor, and bombs falling from that same sky. It seemed incredible and horrible that it should be happening.[11]

With David D. Terry in Washington DC and both Dave Jr. and Bill serving in the military, Terry dealt with the rationing at home as the remaining family joined together to weather the hardships until the end of the conflict.

During this time, Terry worked constantly in the realm of urban development and improvement. She first became involved in urban development in 1939 when she and nine others, including Erle Chambers, formed the Little Rock Housing Association with funds from the 1937 United States Housing Act in an effort to combat slum housing in Little Rock.[12] This act, administered by the United States Public Housing Authority, effectively established the public housing program to award loans to housing agencies (like the Little Rock Housing Association) to be used for the construction of low-rent public housing.[13] Locally, the Arkansas legislature passed legislation in 1937 stating:

> That within the State there is a shortage of safe or sanitary dwelling accommodations available at rents white persons of low incomes can afford and that such persons are forced to occupy overcrowded and congested accommodations, that those conditions necessitate expenditures of public funds for crime prevention and punishment, public health and safety, fire and accident protection, and other public services and facilities; that it is a proper public purpose for any State Public Body to aid, as herein provided, any housing authority operating within its boundaries or jurisdiction or any housing project located therein, as the State Public Body derives immediate benefits and advantages from such an authority or project.[14]

In keeping with this legislation, and after some successful lobbying from Terry and others, the City of Little Rock incorporated the Little Rock Housing Authority in 1940.[15]

Terry also served on the board of the local Urban League, an interracial group dedicated to improving the situation of local African Americans. The Urban League of Greater Little Rock (later the Urban League of Arkansas) was formed by a group of concerned citizens in February 1937 as a branch of the National Urban League. Locally, the group sought to improve the living and working conditions of central Arkansas's African-American population. The organization's board was composed of both white and black members.[16] According to Clifford E. Minton, the first executive officer of the organization, local whites who were willing to serve with the Urban League were "considered ultra liberal."[17] Early work of the Urban League of Greater Little Rock, particularly efforts to improve Gillam

Park, allowed Little Rock to apply for funding when it became available in 1949 after Congress expanded the original housing act. In order to receive the funds, voters had to approve the urban renewal referendum. To help persuade voters, a Committee for Progress was formed with Terry as a co-chair. Terry, foreshadowing later efforts with the WEC, organized an auxiliary women's committee to the group. The twenty-two women involved with the committee spoke on radio programs and to community groups about the importance of "slum clearance and low-rent housing as both an exercise in responsible democracy and a solution to health problems among the poor."[18] The Committee for Progress was successful in its efforts, garnering heavy African-American support and winning the urban renewal election on May 9, 1950. The effort was not without criticism, however, as the planned new housing would contribute to the segregation of Little Rock. During a 1952 action of the Little Rock Housing Authority, many African-American residents opposed the plan to clear ten acres of their homes in the Dunbar High School area, including many substantial homes in addition to slum housing, to build a community center, homes, and apartment buildings. A group of African-American women made a statement about the plan: "We have given almost everything we have ... to pay for these homes, improvements and educate our children. Now for the Housing Authority to come and say we must move away to a much less desirable, convenient and suitable location is far more than we can understand or submit to willingly."[19]

Terry's stint on the board ended when she, with a number of other board members, resigned from the Urban League after Harry Bass, the African-American director, refused to resign when asked to by the board. Bass had operated a lottery, presumably to raise funds for an African-American hospital, and had solicited white politicians. Although many board members returned after a new director was hired, Terry, who was outspoken about her disappointment with the national Urban League and its support of Bass, was not asked to return.[20]

Despite cutting her ties with the Urban League, Terry rarely found herself without a project to work on throughout the 1950s. In particular, she became more involved with the Arkansas Federation of Women's Clubs. The AFWC was formed in 1897 with twenty-five clubs as a charter member and admitted to the General Federation of Women's Clubs the same year.[21] The AFWC provided information, projects, and programs for its member clubs across Arkansas. Terry was involved with the AFWC early on, both through member clubs and while working directly with the main organization. During part of the 1950s, for example, she served as chairman of the United Nations and Specialized Agencies in the Federation's International Affairs Department.[22] As part of her role as chairman, Terry organized a trip to visit the United Nations headquarters to be a capstone for a number of programs about the UN being presented by the various clubs in the Federation. Approximately thirty women signed on for Terry's trip, which cost approximately $100 for a twelve-day tour of various locations in the eastern United States. The first stop for the group was the national meeting of the Federation of Women's Clubs in Philadelphia, Pennsylvania. When the group reached New York City, it toured the United Nations; lunched with Eleanor Roosevelt, who spoke to the group about "promoting interest in the UN"; and visited the traditional tourist locations. On the return trip, the group went through Washington DC and Virginia, visiting the White House; the U.S. Capitol; Arlington National Cemetery; Jamestown; and Arlington House, the home of Robert E. Lee.

Also in the late 1950s, Terry served as fine arts chairman for the Arkansas Federation of Women's Clubs. At a 1956 Board of Directors meeting, AFWC members recommended and approved an exhibit of all forms of art at the 1957 convention, and an art pageant at the 1958 convention."[23] As fine arts chairman, Terry was in charge of this project. According to Terry, when she accepted the appointment as chairman, she "had a plan," as she "had attended a number of artistic productions—an opera, an art show and a symphony, among others. All of them were quite good, but none were well attended and there was no connection among them. It seemed to me that it would be better if these productions were put together and called a festival of the arts or something of that sort, and promoted as a series instead of as individual events."[24] Terry quickly applied her plan to the situation and turned the Federation's desire for an art exhibit into a large festival of the arts.

The first festival was held in Stuttgart, Arkansas, in April of 1957 in conjunction with the AFWC convention. Arkansans submitted more than 250 entries in music, poetry, art, and drama, and winners walked away with the top cash prizes in their categories.[25] Club members in Stuttgart set up three hotel rooms to house the entries and provided members to staff the exhibit.[26] The festival was successful, but Terry was not completely satisfied with the result. In her memoir, she reflected on the project: "I asked a man who was a painter, and whose father and grandfather had been painters, to judge the painting. He was also an art teacher, and he was not a very good judge because he awarded the prizes to people who had been his students. This did not endear him to the local people."[27] Despite her disappointment with the judging, Terry reported back to the AFWC on the success of its new endeavor and the group decided to make the festival an annual event: "Interest shown in our efforts prompted us to continue the project. The Festival will be held in Little Rock next year under the name of the State Art Festival."[28]

At the same time she worked on her projects with the Arkansas Federation of Women's Clubs, Terry had ongoing work as a member of the library system Board of Trustees, including the construction of a new building and the integration of Little Rock public libraries. In 1941, the Urban League of Greater Little Rock sponsored a survey about the resources available to the local African-American population. The resulting *Survey of the Negroes of Little Rock and North Little*

Rock recognized the problems with African-American access to library resources. According to the survey, in 1936, circulation at the Colored Branch Library was 9,709 books compared to 276,995 books at the main public library. The survey attributed this discrepancy among circulation numbers to a lack of funds for acquisition of new books, a lack of leisure time among African-American women, and a lack of organized cultural forces. It recommended an additional librarian for the branch, as well as longer hours, more books on subjects of interest, and "permanent quarters in a quieter neighborhood."[29]

Although the board had discussed the access problem in early 1950, it was not until a letter from Dr. Georg Iggers, a professor from Philander Smith University, was published in the *Arkansas Gazette* that the board directly acted on the problem. The Iggers letter brought community attention to the lack of resources available to his African-American students and questioned the legality of a whites-only library.[30] The main board supporters of integration were Terry, Rabbi Ira Sanders, and J. N. Heiskell.[31] On January 10, 1951, the board approved the partial integration of the main library after a "conference with Negro leaders in the Community." The official resolution read: "First, that the Adult Department of the main library be open to Negroes beginning with students of the seventh grade and to all Negroes over the age of sixteen; Second, that Negroes be required to make application for a library card in the same manner as white patrons."[32] According to Terry, the current library building was too small for total integration, so the board decided to open it up to African-American adults and have the rest of the black population use the branch library until the new building was completed. Construction of the new building was slow, in part because of delays caused by the removal of a decoration at the top of the building that inadvertently looked like a row of swastikas.[33] The Main Library at 7th and Louisiana streets opened to whites and adult African-Americans in 1951, although the Colored Branch Library (renamed the Ivey

Branch in 1953) remained the main library for the black community. The board was not unanimous in its decision to integrate. Terry described one board member's reaction:

> When we decided that we would open the library up to all the adults of the town, black, white and red, one of the members of the Board who didn't want to do it, suggested that we send notices around to the black churches telling people that they should behave like ladies and gentlemen in the library. I asked him who on earth he thought was coming, and what the people were coming for. I felt they were coming to read and take out books, and not to disturb anything or anybody.[34]

Terry was pleased to report that the only disturbance in the new integrated library was caused by a group of children who "interfered with the plumbing and did other damage," prompting the board to employ a security guard for a while.[35]

Later comments by board members claimed that the Iggers letter was not their main motivating factor in the integration. Instead, according to statements made by J. N. Heiskell, the Iggers letter demonstrated the community support for integrating the library that gave the board the extra push it needed to move ahead with its desired plans. Heiskell explained that the trustees had previously believed in the integration of the library but were not sure if the community would support their decision. Over the years, there has been much controversy associated with the real effect of the Iggers letter on the Board of Trustees' decision.[36]

The integration of the public library was a relatively smooth process and gave Terry confidence in the future equality of Little Rock. As she explained:

> We opened the library before there was any real attempt at integration in the community, and we did it very gradually. We said nothing in print about what we were doing, but just did it. I had discovered that if you want to do anything that is different, the people who are most vocal are those who object. You can beat them out of it if

you say nothing in public, but just go ahead. ... As it was, there were no major objects to opening the library, but if we had put a notice in the paper, there doubtless would have been. We did it quietly and I can't remember getting any letters or phone calls objecting to what we had done.[37]

Naturally, Terry applied the lessons she learned during the integration of the library to her work during the Central High desegregation crisis. That situation, however, would be dramatically different for Terry.

Chapter 7

The Central High Crisis and the Women's Emergency Committee

The integration of Little Rock's libraries was just a small step in the ongoing racial change in Arkansas. The local civil rights movement had started to take hold in an organized and supported manner during World War II. One motivating factor for organized protest was the quest of a young lawyer named William Harold Flowers and a court case for equal teacher pay.[1] Flowers hoped to inspire black lawyers throughout Arkansas to implement a plan of action to achieve equality and after being denied financial help from the National Association for the Advancement of Colored People, formed the Committee on Negro Organizations in 1940. By 1942, the CNO was experiencing success and widespread support that fueled the African-American fight for change across the state.[2] Then, in 1942, Arkansas finally entered the courts to fight for civil rights. Sue Cowan Morris, a member of the Little Rock Classroom Teachers Association, sued for black teachers to receive the same salary as their white counterparts. According to historian John Kirk, the case was "the first successful attempt by blacks in Arkansas to win equal rights through the courts."[3] With the established sense of community and belief in the possibility of change, African Americans, especially the influential Little Rock businessmen, joined through a series of actions to push for expanded civil rights in Arkansas.

As Arkansas, and particularly Little Rock, continued to make small steps toward racial equality, the courts stepped in nationally to hasten the process.[4] With the *Brown v. Board of Education of Topeka, Kansas* decision in May 1954, the Supreme Court ruled the "separate but equal" clause that fueled segregation to be unconstitutional. Many believed that Little Rock, viewed as a progressive city at the time, would have a smooth transition to integrated schools. This view of a progressive Little Rock, however, is a whitewashed picture of the metropolitan area. While it is true that some local businesses and officials had taken steps to increase the rights of the African-American population, the city remained largely segregated. As argued by historian Johanna Miller Lewis, "Drinking from the same water fountains and borrowing books from the same library did not add up to racial equality."[5]

Arkansas reacted rapidly to the *Brown* decision with mixed feelings across the state and an assurance of compliance with the law by Governor Francis Cherry. The Little Rock School Board announced its intention to quickly comply with the decision just five days later. It would be a full year later, May of 1955, when the U.S. Supreme Court expanded on compliance requirements for the *Brown* ruling, charging only that states act "with all deliberate speed" and leaving the methods up to individual jurisdictions.

That same month, the Little Rock School Board adopted the Blossom plan of gradual integration. The plan, which was complementary to the widely accepted white view of minimal compliance with the *Brown* decision, had met with mixed reactions from the local branch of the National Association for the Advancement of Colored People. The support of the African-American community was further eroded when the school board continued planning for integration without the input of the NAACP or local African-American residents, who only learned of the developments by word of mouth. Daisy and L. C. Bates described the plan as "vague, indefinite, slow-moving and indicative of an intent to stall further on public school integration."[6]

The Blossom plan called for the first African-American students to enter Little Rock's Central High School at the beginning of the 1957–58 school year. Nine African-American students—Minnijean Brown, Elizabeth Eckford, Ernest Green, Thelma Mothershed, Melba Pattillo, Gloria Ray, Terrence Roberts, Jefferson Thomas, and Carlotta Walls—volunteered and were selected to attend Central High, but the decision met with much protest and increasingly violent resistance.

Terry was encouraged by the school board's initial response to the *Brown* decision and pleased with what she viewed as the social progress of Little Rock:

> I had looked back on the year before [1956] and been greatly encouraged by the cultural and economic progress of Little Rock. The junior college had become Little Rock University and a new symphony orchestra had come into being with the backing of the Chamber of Commerce. The Museum of Natural History and the Fine Arts Museum had both acquired experienced curators, and the Junior League had decided to devote its energies to cultural affairs … we thought that a new day for our city and state had arrived and nothing could stop our progress."[7]

In addition to these cultural events, Little Rock had desegregated its buses and many of its restaurants by this time. Schools elsewhere in Arkansas had already started the process of desegregating. By the time of the events in the fall of 1957, Arkansas had more desegregated public school districts than "nine other southern states combined; the only former Confederate state that had more desegregated schools that Arkansas was Texas."[8] Terry had reason to be optimistic about the future of race relations in the state. As the desegregation of Central High School in the fall of 1957 proceeded, however, Terry was devastated by the violence and anger of the demonstrators.

In an effort to stop the inevitable integration and under the guise of protecting the students from violence, Governor Faubus ordered the National Guard to Central High to prevent the entrance of any African-American students. Faubus's challenge of the authority of the federal government was reminiscent of the southern actions prior to and during the Civil War.[9] It was not until President Eisenhower ordered federal troops, the U.S. Army's 101st Airborne Division, into Little Rock and federalized the Arkansas National Guard that the nine students were able to attend their first full day of classes on September 25, 1957.

Throughout that first year, the Little Rock Nine suffered verbal and physical abuse at the hands of some of their fellow students. Terry reacted to the violence and the circumventing of the law in a particularly disgusted manner, but had mixed feelings about the coming integration:

> In the 1850s the South could not get into the 19th Century without a war, and in the 1950s we cannot get into the 20th. Of course no one wants integration, there are too many problems, but it is here and it is right. For almost 100 years we have taxed ourselves to provide free schools for the negroes and the churches have sent missionaries to carry health, education and religion to the dark people of the world and teach them pride in their humanity; that their immortal souls were of consequence to the Father of us all. The efforts have succeeded but we want the black man to be content with second class citizenship everywhere.[10]

Terry, who was particularly concerned with the way Arkansas was viewed outside of the South, saw the Central High School desegregation crisis as a black spot on the progress of the southern states and as fodder for the communist argument against the United States. She felt that Little Rock "had become a byword for lawlessness and racial hatred all over the world."[11] She was not alone in this thinking. According to historian Karen Anderson, the crisis "threatened [Little Rock's] nascent economic development program" because local businessmen were unwilling to invest in the unstable community.[12] Despite the protests, the school year continued, with Ernest Green, the seniormost member of the group, graduating from Central High in May 1958—the first African-American student to do so. The resistance to desegregation did not decrease, however, and the battle continued in the courts and state government over the summer months as a build-up to a turning point for Arkansas schools.

This event in Arkansas history caused many white Little Rock citizens to view their city as sharply divided among different classes of whites, in addition to the typical white vs. black view. Despite her previous work with people belonging to the underprivileged and economically struggling class, Terry also saw the conflict in this manner: "For almost fifty years, our family had worked for better race relations, and so much had been quietly accomplished. I felt as if my life had been in vain; I really wanted to die. For days I walked about, unable to concentrate on anything, except the fact that we had been disgraced by a group of poor whites and a portion of the lunatic fringe that every town possesses. I wondered where the better class had been while this was being concocted."[13] Early on, poor whites saw the Blossom plan as forcing integration on them as the more affluent whites could send their children to private or suburban schools not yet subjected to the entrance of black students. Unfortunately, despite their insistence that a "lower class" or even outsiders were causing the problems at Central, much of the more affluent or business class were unwilling to jeopardize their position and speak out in favor of integration.[14]

Terry quickly tried to involve herself in the situation by talking to local teachers and community leaders. Early on in the school year, Terry contacted Daisy Bates, president of the local chapter of the NAACP. Daisy Lee Gatson Bates was co-owner with her husband, Lucious Christopher (L. C.) Bates, of the Arkansas State Press, a weekly newspaper focused on African-American civil rights, published beginning in 1941. In 1952, she was elected as president of the Arkansas Conference of Branches of the NAACP. It was in this role that she became active in school desegregation. Although the extent of her role with the Little Rock Nine has been debated by historians, Bates was spokesperson for the NAACP during this time and worked relentlessly for integration. According to historian Grif Stockley, Bates "was in daily contact with the national office of the NAACP in New York as segregationists battled to destroy the NAACP in Arkansas as well as to intimidate her, her husband, and the Little Rock Nine and their families into giving up the struggle."[15]

In April 1958, Terry attended an interracial council meeting to hear about a plan for integration created by Herbert Thomas, who was founder of the First Pyramid Life Insurance Company, president of the University of Arkansas Board of Trustees, and a segregationist. The plan called for the withdrawal of African-American students from Central High School after the 1957–58 school year, followed by the establishment of an interracial commission to develop a voluntary plan for integration. Thomas first introduced his plan on April 7, 1958.[16] According to Terry, the meeting was a success:

> [Thomas] was a clever and political creature, and before the meeting was over he had changed the atmosphere from animosity to good will. The black people present agreed that they wanted an interracial commission to help solve the problems of integration, but none of them were ready to say that they would withdraw their children from Central High and take a "breathing spell," and certainly no one could blame them. For the first time, Herbert Thomas met Mrs. Bates. Both were highly intelligent, and I felt that if the two of them sat down together without any other desire than to work out a solution to the problem they would probably come up with an acceptable answer.[17]

Terry perhaps misread the feelings at the meeting. Bates and Thomas met on April 11, 1958, but his plan never had her support or the support of the African-American community, as Terry suggests. On April 8, following the announcement of the Thomas plan, Bates stated that it would not be endorsed by the NAACP. Thomas did not give up, however, and called a meeting of prominent African-American citizens to argue for his plan. After meeting Bates, Thomas described her as "able and unemotional ... she is uncompromising."

Thomas attributed the failure of his plan to Bates and the NAACP, stating in a letter that while local black leaders were at first accepting of his plan, after the NAACP refused endorsement, "their whole demeanor had changed. They were aloof. They would express no opinion."[18] Terry continued to work with this interracial group, however. Drawing on the experience gained by her previous work with community groups and the Arkansas legislature, Terry suggested having members of the community appointed to a governmental commission by many different organizations to prevent bias. She headed a small committee that decided on a number of organizations to appoint the commission members, but the interracial group felt it was too early to adopt any particular plan, and Terry's work with the group ended.[19]

During this time, Terry also sought to reach out to Governor Faubus through his wife. Terry originally hoped that Faubus would support the desegregation and did not expect him to openly oppose the Supreme Court decision; she had voted for him in the two previous elections. In a letter she wrote to Governor Faubus in November of 1958, Terry remarked:

> I believe that you can be a second Lincoln, but you are now on the wrong path. Lincoln was looking towards the future; you are still looking in the past. The South has no chance of ultimately winning in this matter of segregation. With the election of all the progressive new Democrats there is less chance now than ever before. Whether we like it or not, Segregation around the world is as dead in 1958 as slavery was in 1858. The South cannot afford to fight for lost causes.[20]

Unfortunately, Governor Faubus did not agree with Terry's sentiments. After Faubus's reelection in 1958 when he carried all of Arkansas's seventy-five counties, Terry no longer viewed him as a hopeful choice for the state. She wrote, "All the disturbances at Central High, I felt, had been created by Faubus solely to re-elect himself, and he had succeeded probably beyond his own wildest dreams. I felt he was doing exactly what he would do if he were a communist: fomenting dissension between groups of people and causing intolerance to breed more intolerance. He was working in one of the poorest and most ignorant states, and from it his influence was radiating in all directions."[21] Terry's view of Faubus's actions as a path to reelection was not an unusual take on the situation. According to historian David Chappell, segregationist politician Jim Johnson, defeated by Faubus in the elections, exclaimed, "He used my nickel and hit the jackpot!" while Johnson was "looking sullenly at the overnight sensation who had upstaged him and every other veteran in the segregationist movement."[22]

On September 12, 1958, the U.S. Supreme Court ordered desegregation under the approved plan to continue in Little Rock. Seemingly desperate to remain in control of the situation and prevent a second year of black students in white schools, Governor Faubus took a radical step and closed the Little Rock School District's public high schools—Central High School, Hall High School, Little Rock Technical High School, and Horace Mann High School—on September 15, 1958, to prevent further desegregation until the public voted on the situation. Faubus closed the four schools under the authority granted to him by Act 4. Act 4, approved by the Arkansas legislature with a package of other segregation-related bills in August 1958, allowed the governor to close any or all public schools in Arkansas until a public election could be held to determine the desire for integration. The closing of the schools affected approximately 3,600 students.[23]

In response to the closing of the schools, much of the city remained in shock. Local businessmen who had previously controlled local politics in a non-vocal and detached fashion found their methods ineffective in the political climate of the crisis. These men "were divided over the importance of segregation and over how to safeguard their economic and political interests, their uncertainty left them virtually paralyzed during the first two years of the crisis. Most supported segregation but were unhappy about the high cost of retaining it."[24]

120

The moderate businessmen, unable or unwilling to oppose the segregationists, left a gaping hole of leadership in Little Rock, and many smaller groups were waiting in the wings to fill that void.[25]

It was in this atmosphere that a group of elite white women—Adolphine Fletcher Terry, Vivion Brewer, and Velma Powell—came together on September 12, 1958, to discuss the situation. Previously, Terry had met with Alta Faubus, wife of Governor Orval Faubus, to enlist her help in dissuading the governor from his current plan of action. After this unsuccessful meeting, Terry remained outside of the conflict until a letter from Velma Powell pushed her into action. Powell wrote, "In the past, whenever problems have had to be faced in Little Rock, you have taken a lead in solving them. Why are you silent now?"[26] Powell, thirty-six years old at the time of this meeting and wife of a Central High School vice-principal, had lived in the Terry home for a year while she attended college. Shortly after Terry began testing the water for an organization of women, she received a letter from Powell, secretary of the Arkansas Council on Human Relations, asking why Terry had not stepped up to help the school situation. Terry viewed the letter as perfect timing and contacted Powell, who had made a number of lists of things to help the situation.[27] Vivion Brewer, fifty-seven years old at the time of the meeting, met Terry when she joined the Little Rock branch of the American Association of University Women—the offshoot of Terry's original College Club. Powell suggested to Terry that Brewer would be an appropriate leader, and Terry, having worked for Brewer on the Heiskell dinner, agreed. Brewer did not live in the Little Rock School District, a fact that would later be used by Governor Faubus to try and discount the group, but, like Terry, she was independently wealthy and immune to the possible economic repercussions of their activism. In fact, their status as women provided them with some degree of insulation against economic repercussions in a way that was not the case with their husbands—and businessmen in general.[28]

Confident in their ability to have a positive effect on the crisis, Terry met with Powell and Brewer to form an organization of likeminded women working together for a solution to the education problems in Little Rock—what later became the Women's Emergency Committee to Open Our Schools (WEC). Modeled on the Association of Southern Women for the Prevention of Lynching, the WEC was the first organized white opposition to the segregationists and was "dedicated to the principle of free and public school education, and to law and order. [The WEC members] stand neither for integration nor for segregation, but for education."[29] The WEC aimed to "get the four free public high schools re-opened; to get students back in their classes; to retain our staff of good teachers; [and] to regain full accreditation by the North Central Association."[30] Particularly, the women focused on reopening the schools, with compliance with *Brown* being the only lawful option, regardless of one's personal feelings toward integration. During this first meeting, the brainstorming for the WEC commenced. Vivion Brewer described the feelings of the women this way: "Believing without reservation that all people are far more alike than they are different and that hatred is insanity, we pooled our anxieties. We agreed that it was useless to continue our stunned silence of the past year during which we had waited for the men of affairs to do something." Together, the women created a list of local women who might be willing to join their cause and spent the next weekend calling anyone who "might be induced to come to a meeting designed to organize a study group, an unpublicized gathering to consider the possibilities for influencing the climate of opinion towards racial tolerance."[31]

Fifty-eight women attended the second meeting on September 15, 1958, signing their names on a list as they arrived. At the start of the meeting, Terry spoke about race relations in Arkansas and her desire to create an organization to help strengthen the relationship between white and black. Many of the women in the group were surprised at this turn of events—they were not completely aware of the purpose of the meeting. Several quietly left the meeting, especially as Brewer suggested a number of biracial activities, and three women later asked to have their names taken off the attendance list. The remaining women were less concerned with the larger race relations situation and wanted to focus mainly on the goal of reopening the schools. It was after this meeting that Terry, Brewer, and Powell determined that the WEC could not present itself as pro-integration if it sought to gain acceptance with the public; instead, in an attempt to avoid the larger issue but reach the same end, the WEC would only be presented as a pro-education group seeking to open the schools. It would also be a whites-only organization. Terry, no stranger to biracial activities, was well aware that many of her white supporters would not participate if even a select group of black women were present. To that end, Terry even asked "much-feared radical" Daisy Bates not to attend the meeting. According to historians, this did not sit well with Bates who, in a 1976 interview with historian Elizabeth Jacoway, remarked that she believed that Vivion Brewer wanted "the black community to turn over control of the movement to the white community, to these liberal members of the white community." Bates revealed to Brewer years later that she had written an article against the WEC for its choice of only white membership but did not print it due to her respect for Terry. According to historian Grif Stockley, "A lily-white organization was tactically necessary, though it did not sit well with blacks who were initially sympathetic" to the WEC.[32]

At this first large meeting, the group elected Velma Powell as secretary, Ada Thompson as treasurer, and Vivion Brewer as chairman. Terry had actually asked Powell and Brewer to fill these roles when the three first met. In fact, Brewer arrived at the September 16 meetings with notes written for her new role as chairman. After Terry nominated Brewer for the chairmanship and recounted an extensive list of her accomplishments—making it very clear that she was Terry's choice for the role—the women present at the meeting officially elected her as chairman. Brewer commented on the odd manner in which she was appointed chairman of the WEC—"Quite confused by this railroading and the general purpose, the voters assented and I stood up … making no attempt to be coy about my selection." Powell stepped down as secretary because Terry and Brewer believed that her job as secretary of the Arkansas Council of Human Relations would be polarizing to voters and threaten the image of a moderate WEC; she was replaced by Dottie Morris. During the September 16 meeting, Brewer appointed Hildegard Smith to head a committee to brainstorm a possible name. The group met on September 17 and suggested Women's Emergency Committee to *Save* Our Schools. This was later changed to *Open* Our Schools when the group learned of an organization in New Orleans, Louisiana, using Save Our Schools.[33]

By the September 23 meeting, the number of women meeting in Terry's home jumped to 170.[34] Much of this meeting was spent discussing the activities of the committee that was working on the upcoming school election in which voters would choose segregation or integration. The election was originally set for October 7 but later moved up to September 27, a Saturday when many locals would be in Fayetteville for the Razorbacks football game. WEC member Sara Murphy believed that Faubus changed the election date because he felt the pressure from the WEC and aimed to cut down its planning and response time. Legally, the election was required by Act 4, which Faubus had invoked when he closed the schools. As Terry remarked, the election favored segregationists by calling on voters to vote for or against total "racial integration of all schools within the school district" instead of for the reopening of the Little Rock high schools under the Blossom plan of integration.[35] The election committee, headed by WEC secretary Dottie Morris, recruited volunteers for four projects: 1) contacting eligible voters by phone using names from the poll tax book, 2) driving people to the polls to vote, 3) holding Coca-Cola parties, and 4) watching the polls.[36] Showing the WEC's importance in the community, the *U.S. News* sent a photographer to photograph the women at this third meeting. Many of these early pictures of the group were not published, due, according to Brewer, to the age of those pictured. Patronizingly called "nice old ladies" by the segregationist White Citizens' Council, the gray-haired women did not have the image reporters wanted to propagate. One reporter even told a WEC member that he considered taking "a picture of a very pretty young girl on the Capitol grounds and try[ing] to run it nationally as the leader of the WEC." Later, the WEC used younger women for photo opportunities and to visit the legislature, a trick learned by Terry during her time in the suffrage movement. Irene Samuel, who became the executive secretary of the WEC in May of 1959, was in charge of recruiting and training the women who lobbied for education in the legislature. According to historian Laura Miller, Samuel understood that "some male legislators, however, were uncomfortable because many of the women were better informed than they were. Samuel decided that the best way to ensure that the men would listen was to select young, attractive [WEC] members to lead the lobbying effort."[37]

A membership survey taken by the WEC in 1960 shows that the organization attracted women not considered the "average" Arkansan. According to the survey results, of the members responding, nearly half were between the ages of thirty-seven to fifty, and eighty percent were married. Remarkably, twenty percent of the women had graduated from college, with twenty-one percent of those doing some type of graduate work. Forty-one percent had taken at least some college; only three percent reported not finishing high school.[38] In addition, the income levels of WEC members were in stark contrast with the earnings of general Arkansans, the latter earning less than half of the average WEC wages in 1959. Compare WEC incomes with just those of white Americans and the number is still thirty-three percent higher.[39] The make-up of the membership, while remarkable, is not unexpected; these kinds of women had the free time and resources to work with the WEC. Neither is it unusual that women banded together to enter politics; as discussed earlier, women often used issues related to children and education as their window into activism, a natural extension of their role in the home. Women who were willing to speak up during the Central High Crisis had to work against the stereotypical feminine image of "Mother in the kitchen, tending traditional values along with the home fires."[40] Members of WEC were willing to make the difficult jump into the public domain. Many, like Terry, had previous experience with activism. Given that the members conformed "to traditional patterns of women's reform movements," the WEC found itself in "a uniquely powerful position in the fall of 1958."[41] Still, the women faced outrage and threats from the public, with Terry particularly a target due to her strong southern heritage as the daughter of a Confederate veteran.

In preparation for the school election, the WEC hosted a televised panel discussion on September 25, 1958. Although WEC members approached all three local news channels, only KATV allowed the women any airtime to refute a September 18 televised speech by Faubus. (The other two local channels later denied that the WEC had ever inquired about a segment, and they allowed the group to purchase airtime.) In his speech, Faubus spoke of the violence and lowering of educational standards that would follow integration, allowing his plan to replace the public high schools with private schools as the only possible solution. In their broadcast, the members of the WEC-sponsored panel—Margaret Stephens, Ed Lester, John E. Coates, Rev. Dale Cowling, Marguerite Henry, and moderator William Hadley Jr.—argued against the Faubus plan and urged viewers to vote *for* integration in the September 27 election. A second panel composed of ministers and held on the eve of the election was not as successful, as Bishop Robert R. Brown had attempted to back out just before airtime when he became concerned about alienating his parishioners and had to be coerced into participating. Terry was "very much disappointed in our Bishop who spoke in the most glittering generalities."[42]

One very important goal of these broadcasts was to convince the members of the public not to be afraid of voting for integration, because they were only voting for the previously agreed on Blossom plan. The wording on the ballot, however, caused many Arkansans to believe they were voting for total and immediate integration. Notably, the WEC was careful not to come out in support of integration in an effort to avoid alienating possible supporters and losing members. As Terry explained, "If people had asked any of us if we were for integration, we would probably have told them no, we hadn't come to that point yet. But we were for integrating the schools because there had never been enough money in Arkansas for one good school system, let alone two."[43] When asked by an Associated Press reporter whether or not she supported integration, Brewer replied that "we are not concerned with this," but she experienced "personal guilt for the quote." Terry later admitted to a reporter that she was an integrationist, but for the most part, the WEC officially maintained that it was pro-education and not pro-integration and was operating only because it came down to integrated schools or no schools.[44]

This strategy did not help the WEC, as the group was fighting a losing battle. Little Rock voted *against* reopening the school 19,470 to 7,565 votes. The schools remained empty for the entire 1958–59 school year after a federal injunction blocked Faubus from enacting his plan to open private schools in the public school buildings (although the football season continued uninterrupted), and some 600 high school seniors, mostly African American, received no educational instruction, as they were unable to find an alternative.[45] Parents and students scrambled to find alternative programs. Many students lived with relatives elsewhere in the state or moved to different states entirely. Others, particularly the white students, attended the many private—and segregated—schools in Little Rock or entered the local colleges early without a high school diploma.

Many WEC members, including Terry, and others in Little Rock who supported the reopening of the schools experienced harassment and hardship from their opponents in the community. In her autobiography, Terry refers to these times as "shocking and horrible days." She gives the example of Dr. Dunbar Ogden, who "was one of the few clergymen who acted according to his beliefs. He made no bones about expressing his opinions."[46] Ogden, a white minister who had served at Central Presbyterian Church since 1954 and was president of the newly formed Interracial Ministerial Alliance, had been called upon by Daisy Bates during the 1957–58 school year to gather a group of ministers willing to escort the Little Rock Nine. According to historian Dave Chappell, "Though Ogden became a committed integrationist after this experience … he first felt a simple duty to offer whatever protection his presence among them might afford the children." Ogden contacted a number of clergy members, and most declined his plea for assistance. In the end, Ogden escorted the children along with his son, David, who served as his "bodyguard," white ministers Colby Cartwright, Will D. Campbell, and George A. Chauncey, and black ministers Z. Z. Dryver and Harry Bass. Later, Ogden released a manifesto through the Interracial Ministerial Alliance supporting desegregation. This manifesto greatly alienated his parishioners, and attendance to his sermons decreased. Ogden eventually resigned and moved to West Virginia, and Terry never saw him again. David Ogden, who had accompanied his father while escorting the Nine, stayed in Little Rock and faced the persecution previously directed toward his father; he committed suicide in 1960.[47]

Although these are extreme examples of the hardships encountered by supporters of integration, Terry herself once had an anonymous caller threaten to burn her house down. Terry presented some excerpts from letters she received in her autobiography.

Some writers loathed her actions—

You will regret that one day you favored integration. I was borned in the South, I cant imagine a Southener upholding integration. Truly there must have been brainwashing by some source. This mixing of the races is not God's plan for the Anglo Saxon race.

The good Lord never intended the two races to mix—not any more than he did for animals and birds to mix—uneducated they know what is right and wrong. When you realize that 78% of Washington, D.C. schools are Negroes, it makes one shudder to think what may happen here. If you give a Negro an inch he will take a mile ... Mind you, I'm for Negroes having equal schools, but let them stay in their own.

Listen Mrs. Terry—Vassar. What a fake—you are more than the Governor said of you—all for the worse—1300 of these here Cards to be mailed about these facts on you—the Pond and Your brother and Your Family—The search light on you will uncover worse—A Vet neighbor who knows all.

I have know and been a friend of your family for many a year. You would know me better as a close friend of your husband. Needless to say I just haven't the gall to tell you who I am. You will feel the effect of my work against you in the very near future.

Other letters were supportive—

The bitter, lying words which Our Leader has thrown at you only add evidence to that which already exists, that he is a man of small caliber and low breeding. His attack will not hurt you among the people who know you and Mr. Terry, or among those who know of the long years of service the two of you have given our state.

My grandfather sat in the legislature at Little Rock and voted as he thought for States rights—well our family learned a lesson—because grandfather and 6 brothers in law were killed in the civil war—as far as I am concerned—the union of the states is supreme to the individual state.

But what gets my pride is this—that after all the years in America—with all the freedom as compared to Europe—that now my people of Arkansas fear the competition of the emancipated blacks who have only had their freedom 90 or 100 years.

This whole school affair has been a disgrace to the state and to the Christian people of our nation. I am so glad you and your co-workers have had the nerve and the public spirit to assert yourself and lead out in a movement to get the children back into school. The children are the ones who have really suffered. I believe they could do a much better job running school affaires than some adults.
Why have so many people of the state bowed to the dictatorship of one person and his cohorts? It is amazing.

The Board of Directors of the Young Women's Christian Association of Hot Springs voted in our regular monthly meeting ... to send this letter to you and to the "Women's Emergency Committee to Open Our Schools" to inform you of our appreciation of your stand as regards the integration issue and the special school election ... in Little Rock.[48]

Although they lost the first election, the WEC members continued to push for the reopening of the schools and the continuation of the desegregation plan, experiencing most of their success after the initial election through extensive lobbying and grassroots work. On November 10, 1958, the U.S. Eighth Circuit Court of Appeals placed an injunction against the use of public school buildings for private instruction and ordered the district to continue with its integration plan, prompting five of the six school board members to resign two days later, citing their situation as "utter hopelessness, helplessness, and frustration." The resulting December 6 regular election included candidates supported by the WEC and left the board with stalemate membership make-up of three moderates and three segregationists. The board butted heads over the renewal of teacher contracts, leading to a walk-out of the moderate members and the firing of a large number of school employees by the segregationist members. This action promoted local businessmen to finally take a stand against the segregationists and form Stop This Outrageous Purge (STOP). The organizations worked together to obtain and check 9,603 signatures (more than the

7,500 minimum) to hold a recall election for the School Board members. The results of a May 25 election placed three moderate members on the board and ousted three segregationist members. The new moderate Little Rock School Board then set out to reopen the schools and reestablish the process of gradual desegregation.[49]

After the initial formation and actions of the WEC, Terry—at least as outsiders saw it—stepped back from the WEC into an almost advisory role, lending the group her name, credibility, and resources while leaving Brewer to lead the group in her role as chairman. When Brewer resigned from this role in 1960, a conversation between her and Jo Jackson reveals the position of both Brewer and Terry within the WEC. Brewer informed Jackson that she would be resigning and leaving Pat House as chairman, but Jackson believed that House was already chairman and remarked, "I thought you were just like Mrs. Terry—just there!" This is not to say, however, that WEC members disliked Terry. On the contrary, Terry was well respected and looked up to by much of the group.[50]

On November 2, 1963, the WEC voted itself out of existence after a decrease in membership and activity as the women moved on to other political organizations. The WEC had served its immediate purpose of working for the stabilization of Arkansas education and had "brought its women to an alert realization of problems, had taught them the need for and the value of their concern," creating a new group of women activists to work for their community. As it disbanded, the group presented Terry with a plaque that read: "In deep appreciation for your unique, selfless and unremitting contribution to humanity and for your inspiration and guidance to the Women's Emergency Committee."[51]

The success of the Women's Emergency Committee was the capstone of Adolphine Fletcher Terry's lifetime commitment to social activism. When the iconic photograph of Terry standing below the image of her Confederate father appeared in *Time* magazine, she received a letter from the president of Vassar College, which read, "I want you to know how greatly I admire you and how glad I am that Vassar may claim you for one of her own. Need I say that I hope your Vassar education helped to forward the tenets of good citizenship for which you stand."[52] Although the women "did not overtly depart from traditional patterns of female behavior"[53] and operated within the constraints placed on elite southern white women during their time as WEC members, through their commitment they "played a central role in toppling traditional constructions of gender as well as race in Little Rock." Historian Elizabeth Jacoway places the importance of the WEC higher than simply its fight for Arkansas education, contending that Terry's actions, "had the unexpected consequences of freeing white women as well ... it is clear that in giving Little Rock's elite women a public voice, in teaching them to think in terms of political organizing and acting, they led the way toward a new understanding of female possibilities in their city. In the years after the WEC ceased operations, the women Brewer and Terry had trained remained active in a broad range of public pursuits in Little Rock and elsewhere."[54] Although not all of the WEC members had previously lacked the qualities and experience necessary to hold active roles in community and politics, many of the women were entering activism for the first time and looked to Terry and other experienced WEC members for guidance. Since her work with the school system in the early 1900s, Terry, aided by her status as an elite woman, demonstrated a willingness to challenge and expand the role of women in society while working within the socially imposed boundaries in a non-confrontational manner. With a talent for listening to those around her and an ability to use her perceived position as a southern elite white woman to her advantage, Terry succeeded in championing a moderate position on race and gender while working for the betterment of the lives of all Arkansans.

Conclusion

After Terry's work with the WEC, she continued to be active in Arkansas, but she did not assume a large role in any project like those discussed here, preferring instead to leave the work to "younger people, or at least people with more energy."[1] In 1961, Vassar College chose Terry as one of its 100 distinguished graduates in honor of the school's centennial celebration. Terry was chosen because she had "the intelligence to balance tradition and change" and "the generosity to give of oneself and one's understanding to make a better world in which to live."[2] In 1964, Terry worked with Annie Mae Bankhead to start an African-American Head Start program in College Station, Arkansas, and followed it up by helping to raise $22,000 for a community center five years later.[3] Looking back on her life, Terry reminisced:

> Although I never worked for wages, throughout my life I have always found work to do, or it has found me. I don't know whether it was all good or necessary work, but I did it and enjoyed it. In fact, I have enjoyed all of my life, and at the age of ninety one I do not fear death … I have felt for a long time that by working on things and trying to make them better, and thereby make life better, a person is in some way speeding up the development of himself and of mankind."[4]

Her contributions were not overlooked by her friends and acquaintances. In 1966, Terry was honored by a tribute sponsored by the Arkansas Council on Human Relations that was attended by 500 people.[5] In his speech at the event, Harry S. Ashmore remarked on Terry's importance to Arkansas:

> It is quite literally true that I could fill my allotted time and do great honor to Adolphine Terry simply by reciting the astonishing list of her accomplishments. … Education, as the *Gazette* suggested, is the lodestone of her interests, but her commitment is by no means exclusive. She is a formidable figure in the Episcopal church, and in all the cultural affairs of the city and state; her imprint can be found

on every charitable organization and upon the public welfare agencies; she was a personal force in state and national politics during the years David Terry served in Congress, and after; and we know only a few of the benefactions she has privately bestowed upon the young and hopeful, and the old and despairing. These concerns reach to the ultimate limits of the community. In their pursuit Adolphine Terry came early to confront the peculiar institutions that have set Southerners apart, and truncated the aspirations of whites and Negroes alike. ... In the beginning she worked of necessity within the bounds of Southern caste. ... Sooner or later her unmistakable competence brought her to membership on the boards of all the major charities and civic enterprises, and there she functioned as an early-day ombudsman. ... we recall another June ... when a determined young woman came home from Vassar College to unfurl the bright banner of courage and hope she has followed all her extraordinary life.[6]

In his speech, Ashmore focused on Terry's work with African-American groups and her desire for better race relations. When commenting on her philosophy regarding race relations, Terry said, "I see no reason to pay any more attention to the color of a person's skin than to the color of his eyes. It's so much easier to speak to a person merely as another person than to put on a different voice and a different face for someone of another color."[7] This belief can easily been seen throughout Terry's life, particularly in her willingness to be involved with projects like the Phyllis Wheatley YWCA. Later, in 1971, Terry was again recognized by her community. At the eighth annual Brotherhood Citation dinner of the Arkansas Region of the National Conference of Christians and Jews, Terry—along with J. N. Heiskell, owner and editor of the *Arkansas Gazette*—was honored with the Brotherhood Award.[8]

Adolphine Fletcher Terry died in Little Rock, Arkansas, on July 25, 1976, at the age of ninety-three and is buried in Mount Holly Cemetery in Little Rock. She had committed her life to Arkansas, a place she once described as "holy ground."[9] Terry left a long and successful legacy in Arkansas and was recognized by the local media for her efforts. In the *Arkansas Gazette*, Terry was described as a "lady and true heroine, one who left the imprint of her spirit, her character, her intellect, upon the 20th century history of Arkansas" and as "one of the leading Arkansans of her time." The article went on to say that she "was a magnificent figure and her record will adorn the histories of our state. In any state it is only once in, let us say, a hundred years, that an Adolphine Terry comes along, and the lives of all of us are enriched for her coming."[10]

Terry was a southern white aristocrat, the daughter of a Confederate soldier who lived her day-to-day life immersed in southern stereotypes, and a fiercely independent and confident woman who dedicated her life to others. Terry had many motives behind her social activism. She worked for school consolidation to relieve her boredom as she waited to marry and to fulfill a perceived obligation due to her class and education. Terry worked with the American Legion Auxiliary and, in some sense, the juvenile court, as part of her duties as a congressman's wife. Later, she involved herself in the tumultuous Central High School desegregation crisis because of an overwhelming interest in the well-being of those around her. She was in many ways a stereotypical southern elite, but she was also a strong and intelligent woman who was committed to creating a more egalitarian world for those Arkansans who were not in a position to help themselves. Harry Ashmore once remarked of Terry, "Her operating assumption is that most of us, black or white, are better than we usually have a chance to be. She may even believe, in the face of all the evidence, that love will ultimately triumph."[11] But perhaps Terry said it best herself: "We are bound to accept this responsibility. ... We are obliged to help them."[12]

Notes

Introduction:

1. Bob Besom, "The Springdale Meeting of the Arkansas Historical Association, 2000," *Arkansas Historical Quarterly* 59 (Autumn 2000): 316.

2. *Arkansas Times*, December 31, 1999.

3. *Arkansas Gazette*, June 26, 1976.

4. Vivion Brewer, *The Embattled Ladies of Little Rock, 1958–1963: The Struggle to Save Public Education at Central High* (Fort Bragg, CA: Lost Coast Press, 1998); Peggy Harris, "Adolphine Fletcher Terry," *The Encyclopedia of Arkansas History & Culture*, http://www.encyclopediaofarkansas.net/encyclopedia/entry-detail.aspx?search=1&entryID=1779; Sara Alderman Murphy, *Breaking the Silence: Little Rock's Women's Emergency Committee to Open Our Schools, 1958–1963* (Fayetteville: University of Arkansas Press, 1997); *Arkansas Democrat*, March 3, 1947; *Arkansas Gazette*, May 9, 1971; *Arkansas Gazette*, June 26, 1976.

5. Harry Ashmore, "Adolphine Fletcher Terry" (speech, Adolphine Terry Dinner, Arkansas Council on Human Relations, Little Rock, AR, June 14, 1966).

6. Nancy Williams, ed., *Arkansas Biography: A Collection of Notable Lives* (Fayetteville: University of Arkansas Press, 2000); Harris, "Adolphine Fletcher Terry."

7. John Gould Fletcher, *Life is My Song* (New York: AMS Press, 1937). Terry, who had a strained relationship with her brother, is not mentioned by name in his autobiography, but she occasionally appears when Fletcher refers to "my sisters" or "my sister."

8. Letter to William L. Terry from Carolyn Rose, Quapaw Quarter Association Records, Butler Center for Arkansas Studies, Arkansas Studies Institute, Little Rock, AR.

9. Brewer, *Embattled Ladies*; Murphy, *Breaking the Silence*.

10. Henry M. Alexander, *The Little Rock Recall Election* (New York: McGraw-Hill, 1960); Lorraine Gates, "Power from the Pedestal: The Women's Emergency Committee and the Little Rock School Crisis," *Arkansas Historical Quarterly* 55 (Spring 1996): 26–57; Elizabeth Jacoway, *Turn Away Thy Son: Little Rock, the Crisis That Shocked the Nation* (Fayetteville: University of Arkansas Press, 2007).

11. Diane Fowlkes, *White Political Women: Paths From Privilege To Empowerment*, (Knoxville: University of Tennessee Press, 1992); Elna C. Green, *Southern Strategies: Southern Women and the Woman Suffrage Question* (Chapel Hill: University of North Carolina Press, 1997); Gail S. Murray, ed., *Throwing Off the Cloak of Privilege: White Southern Women Activists in the Civil Rights Era* (Gainesville: University of Florida Press, 2004).

12. David L. Chappell, "Diversity within a Racial Group: White People in Little Rock, 1957–1959," *Arkansas Historical Quarterly* 54 (Winter 1995): 444–56; Janie Synatzske Evins, "Arkansas Women: Their Contributions to Society, Politics, and Business, 1865–1900," *Arkansas Historical Quarterly* 44

(1985): 118–33; Frances Mitchell Ross, "The New Woman as Club Woman and Social Activist in Turn of the Century Arkansas," *Arkansas Historical Quarterly* 50 (Winter 1991): 317–51.

 13. *Arkansas Gazette*, June 27, 1976.

Chapter 1:

 1. Adolphine Fletcher Terry, "Life is My Song, Also," Unpublished Manuscript, Fletcher-Terry Papers, University of Arkansas at Little Rock Archives at the Arkansas Studies Institute, Little Rock, AR, 1–2. (Hereafter referred to as the Terry Manuscript).

 2. Terry Manuscript, 2.

 3. Terry Manuscript, 45.

 4. Terry Manuscript, 4–5.

 5. Terry Manuscript, 7.

 6. Terry Manuscript, 12. Fletcher served two terms as mayor of Little Rock and unsuccessfully ran for governor of Arkansas three times.

 7. Terry Manuscript, 8.

 8. Terry Manuscript, 3.

 9. Ben F. Johnson, "By Accident of Birth": John Gould Fletcher and Refashioning the Southern Identity," *Arkansas Historical Quarterly* 52 (Spring 1994): 7.

 10. Terry Manuscript, 14, 35–36, 42. The fear of kidnapping perhaps began when a young boy from wealthy parents, Charlie Ross, was kidnapped for ransom and never seen again. Adolphine Fletcher Terry, *Cordelia: Member of the Household.* (Fort Smith, AR: South and West, Inc., 1967): 13.

 11. Terry Manuscript, 14.

 12. Terry Manuscript, 38–39.

 13. Terry Manuscript, 39.

 14. Carl H. Moneyhon, *Arkansas and the New South, 1874–1929* (Fayetteville: University of Arkansas Press, 1997), 41.

 15. Terry Manuscript, 11–12.

 16. Terry Manuscript, 15.

 17. Terry Manuscript, 40.

 18. Terry, *Cordelia*, 18.

 19. Terry Manuscript, 43.

 20. Terry Manuscript, 42.

 21. Sara Alderman Murphy, *Breaking the Silence: Little Rock's Women's Emergency Committee to Open Our Schools, 1958–1963* (Fayetteville: University of Arkansas Press, 1997), 5.

 22. Terry, *Cordelia*, 3.

 23. Terry, *Cordelia*, 108.

 24. Terry, *Cordelia*, 17.

 25. Terry Manuscript, 48–49.

 26. Terry Manuscript, 49.

27. Terry Manuscript, 50.

28. Terry Manuscript, 55.

29. Letter from Adolphine Fletcher Terry to David D. Terry, July 5, 1924, Fletcher-Terry Papers, UALR Archives at the ASI.

30. Terry Manuscript, 57.

31. Vassar College, http://www.vassar.edu; Emily Anne Langdon, "A Study of the Persistence of Affective Outcomes of Women's College Alumnae" (PhD diss., University of California, Los Angeles, 1997), 13, 15.

32. Terry Manuscript, 59.

33. John Gould Fletcher Jr. left Harvard without a degree and went on to become one of Arkansas's most notable literary figures, receiving the 1939 Pulitzer Prize for Poetry. Suffering from mental illness for most of his life, Fletcher drowned himself in 1950.

34. Naturally, many Arkansans have attended Vassar College since Martin and Terry's time there, some due in part to the encouragement from an example set by Terry and others like her. In a letter to Terry, Harry Ashmore exclaimed, "I have told my daughter Anna that if Vassar does one-tenth as well by her as it (or something) has done by you I will consider my investment worthwhile." Letter from Harry Ashmore to Adolphine Fletcher Terry, July 1, 1966, Fletcher-Terry Papers, UALR Archives at the ASI.

35. Terry Manuscript, 58.

36. Terry Manuscript, 58–59.

37. Letter from Adolphine Fletcher Terry to David D. Terry, June 19, 1924, Fletcher-Terry Papers, UALR Archives at the ASI.

38. Terry Manuscript, 61.

39. Terry Manuscript, 61–62.

40. Terry Manuscript, 87.

41. Terry Manuscript, 61, 63.

42. Terry Manuscript, 62.

43. Terry Manuscript, 66.

44. Terry Manuscript, 66–67.

45. Terry Manuscript, 67.

46. Elna C. Green, *Southern Strategies: Southern Women and the Woman Suffrage Question* (Chapel Hill: University of North Carolina Press, 1997), 6.

47. Green, *Southern Strategies*, 16.

48. Mikyong Minsun Kim, "Institutional Effectiveness of Women-Only Colleges: Cultivating Students' Desire to Influence Social Conditions," *Journal of Higher Education* 72 (May–June 2001): 291.

49. Kim, "Institutional Effectiveness," 311.

50. Green, *Southern Strategies*, 15.

51. Terry Manuscript, 60–61.

52. Terry Manuscript, 59.

53. Kim, "Institutional Effectiveness," 290.

54. Kim, "Institutional Effectiveness," 287.

55. Terry Manuscript, 72.

Chapter 2:

1. Terry Manuscript, 86.

2. Terry Manuscript, 87.

3. Terry Manuscript, 88.

4. Terry Manuscript, 72.

5. Terry Manuscript, 91.

6. Terry Manuscript, 92.

7. Terry Manuscript, 72, 75.

8. Terry Manuscript, 76–77.

9. Terry Manuscript, 79–80.

10. *Arkansas Gazette*, July 28, 1972.

11. Terry Manuscript, 81.

12. Frances Mitchell Ross, "The New Woman as Club Woman and Social Activist in Turn of the Century Arkansas," *Arkansas Historical Quarterly* 50 (Winter 1991): 319.

13. Ross, "The New Woman," 320.

14. Cheryl Hyde, "Experiences of Women Activists: Implications for Community Organizing Theory and Practice," *Journal of Sociology and Social Welfare* 13 (1986): 547.

15. Emily Anne Langdon, "A Study of the Persistence of Affective Outcomes of Women's College Alumnae" (PhD diss., University of California, Los Angeles, 1997), 28.

16. Mikyong Minsun Kim, "Institutional Effectiveness of Women-Only Colleges: Cultivating Students' Desire to Influence Social Conditions," *Journal of Higher Education* 72 (May–June 2001): 291.

17. Terry Manuscript, 95–96.

18. *Arkansas Gazette*, July 26, 1976.

19. American Association of University Women, Arkansas Division, "History, Arkansas Division, American Association of University Women" (1947): 77–79.

20. *Arkansas Gazette*, May 9, 1971.

21. College Club Constitution, American Association of University Women Collection, University of Arkansas at Little Rock Archives at the Arkansas Studies Institute, Little Rock, AR.

22. College Club Constitution, AAUW Collection.

23. Marilyn Gittell, Isolda Ortege-Bustamante, and Tracy Steffy, *Women Creating Social Capital and Social Change: A Study of Women-led Community Development Organizations* (New York: Howard Samuels State Management and Policy Center, 1999), 3, 61.

24. Frances Mitchell Ross, "The New Woman as Club Woman and Social Activist in Turn of the Century Arkansas," *Arkansas Historical Quarterly* 50 (Winter 1991): 319.

25. Stephen Weeks, *History of Public Education in Arkansas* (Washington DC: Government Printing Office, 1912), 78.

26. William Wilson, "History of Public School Education in Arkansas, 1900–1918" (MA thesis, University of Chicago, 1918), 45.

27. Weeks, *History of Public Education*, 78.

28. Wilson, "History of Public School Education," 45.

29. Arkansas Department of Education, "Eighteenth Biennial Report of the Superintendent of Public Instruction of the State of Arkansas, 1903–1904" (Arkansas: Central Printing Company, 1904): 12–13.

30. Arkansas Department of Education, "Nineteenth Biennial Report of the Superintendent of Public Instruction of the State of Arkansas, 1905–1906" (Arkansas: Central Printing Company, 1906): 29.

31. Arkansas Department of Education, "Seventeenth Biennial Report of the Superintendent of Public Instruction of the State of Arkansas, 1901–1902" (Arkansas: Central Printing Company, 1902): 18.

32. ADE, "Seventeenth Biennial Report," 18–19.

33. ADE, "Eighteenth Biennial Report," 13.

34. ADE, "Nineteenth Biennial Report," 30.

35. Terry Manuscript, 82.

36. Terry Manuscript, 82.

37. Fred W. Allsopp, ed., *The Poets and Poetry of Arkansas* (Little Rock: Central Printing Company, 1933), 145. Clio Harper was the publisher and editor of multiple publications. He was secretary of the Arkansas Press Association for twenty-six years and was professionally associated with the *Arkansas Democrat* in Little Rock, Arkansas, from 1893 to 1911. In 1911, Harper served as one of twenty-two members of the Arkansas Education Commission. This commission was financed by the Southern Education Board (financed by the Rockefeller family) to study Arkansas education and led to the establishment of the Arkansas Board of Education. William Wilson, "History of Public School Education in Arkansas," 101.

38. Terry Manuscript, 83.

39. Terry Manuscript, 83.

40. Terry Manuscript, 84.

41. ADE, "Eighteenth Biennial Report," 19.

42. Weeks, *History of Public Education*, 79–83.

43. Terry Manuscript, 84.

44. Weeks, *History of Public Education*, 111.

45. Dallas T. Herndon, ed., *Centennial History of Arkansas*, vol. 1 (Little Rock, AR: S. J. Clarke Publishing Company, 1922), 548; Weeks, *History of Public Education*, 111–12.

46. Weeks, *History of Public Education*, 111.

47. Nancy Abrahams, "Negotiating Power, Identity, Family, and Community," *Gender and Society* 10 (1996): 784.

48. Abrahams, "Negotiating Power," 781–82.

49. Harry Ashmore, "Adolphine Fletcher Terry" (speech, Adolphine Terry Dinner, Arkansas Council on Human Relations, Little Rock, AR, June 14, 1966).

Chapter 3:

1. Terry Manuscript, 95.

2. Terry Manuscript, 96

3. David Terry and Adolphine Fletcher Marriage License, Fletcher-Terry Papers, University of Arkansas at Little Rock Archives at the Arkansas Studies Institute, Little Rock, AR; Terry Manuscript, 94.

4. Terry Manuscript, 97.

5. Terry Manuscript, 97.

6. "FABCO to Restore Historic Structure," Quapaw Quarter Association Records, Butler Center for Arkansas Studies, Arkansas Studies Institute, Little Rock, AR.

7. Terry Manuscript, 99–100.

8. "FABCO," Quapaw Quarter Association Records, Butler Center; Terry Manuscript, 99.

9. Mary Louise Terry was born in 1901. She followed in Terry's footsteps and attended Vassar College after high school. Letter from David D. Terry to William L. Terry, March 30, 1915, Fletcher-Terry Papers, UALR Archives at the ASI.

10. Terry Manuscript, 102.

11. Terry Manuscript, 102.

12. Diary of the First Years of David D. Terry Jr., Fletcher-Terry Papers, UALR Archives at the ASI.

13. Terry Manuscript, 118B.

14. Calvin R. Ledbetter, *Carpenter from Conway: George Washington Donaghey as Governor of Arkansas 1909–1913* (Fayetteville: University of Arkansas Press, 1993), 4.

15. Ledbetter, *Carpenter from Conway*, 7.

16. Carl H. Moneyhon, *Arkansas and the New South, 1874–1929* (Fayetteville: University of Arkansas Press, 1997), 115.

17. Moneyhon, *Arkansas and the New South*, 120–21.

18. Dorothy and Carl J. Schneider, *American Women in the Progressive Era, 1900–1920* (New York: Facts on File, 1993), 11.

19. Marilyn Isolda Gittell, et al., *Women Creating Social Capital and Social Change: A Study of Women-led Community Development Organizations* (New York: Howard Samuels State Management and Policy Center, 1999), 3.

20. Anne Firor Scott, *Making the Invisible Woman Visible* (Urbana, IL: University of Illinois Press, 1984), 219.

21. Kathleen L. Hinga, "Women's Local Community Activism: Paths to Politicization" (PhD diss., Boston University, 2005), 1.

22. Moyers, "Arkansas Progressivism," 414–15, 564.

23. Ellen Ryerson, *The Best-Laid Plans: America's Juvenile Court Experiment* (New York: Hill and Wang, 1978), 3.

24. Ryerson, *The Best-Laid Plans*, 3, 15.

25. Ryerson, *The Best-Laid Plans*, 32.

26. Frances Mitchell Ross, "The New Woman as Club Woman and Social Activist in Turn of the Century Arkansas," *Arkansas Historical Quarterly* 50 (Winter 1991): 342.

27. Ross, "The New Woman as Club Woman," 328.

28. Public Acts of Arkansas § 215 (1911).

29. Ross, "The New Woman as Club Woman," 342; Mrs. Kermit W. Toombs, "History of Pulaski County Juvenile Administration Center" (MA thesis, Arkansas State Teachers College, 1964), 3.

30. Toombs, "History," 4.

31. Terry Manuscript, 103.

32. Mattie Cal Maxted, "Some Problems of Court for Children in Arkansas," *Arkansas Law Review* 9 (1954–1955): 23–24; T. James McDonough, "The Juvenile Court and Judicial Reform in Arkansas," *Arkansas Law Review* 22 (1968–1969): 18.

33. Public Acts of Arkansas § 215 (1911).

34. Public Acts of Arkansas § 215 (1911).

35. Terry Manuscript, 103–4.

36. Terry Manuscript, 103.

37. Toombs, "History," 4; *Arkansas Gazette*, February 21, 1937; Public Acts of Arkansas § 215 (1911).

38. Terry Manuscript, 104–5.

39. Toombs, "History," 4; Terry Manuscript, 105–6.

40. Toombs, 5–6; *Arkansas Gazette*, February 21, 1917.

41. Toombs, 5–6; *Arkansas Gazette*, February 14, 1937; *Arkansas Gazette*, February 21, 1917.

42. Terry Manuscript, 107.

43. Public Acts of Arkansas § 199 (1905).

44. Ross, 343.

45. Herndon, *Centennial*, 437.

46. Erle Chambers, "Correctional Institutions," in *Arkansas and Its People: A History, 1541–1930*, ed. David Yancey Thomas (New York: The American Historical Association, 1930), 503.

47. Chambers, "Correctional Institutions," 505. In 1919, the legislature established a second institution, the Arkansas State Farm for Women, which opened in 1920. Terry served on its original board.

48. Chambers, "Correctional Institutions," 503; Herndon, *Centennial*, 438.

49. Chambers, "Correctional Institutions," 503–4; Terry Manuscript, 108.

50. Terry is referring to Tom Jefferson Terral, governor of Arkansas from 1925 to 1927.

51. Terry Manuscript, 109.

52. Maxted, "Some Problems of Court," 24.

53. Letter to Dr. Kelvin M. Mitchell, February 3, 1969, Fletcher-Terry Papers, UALR Archives at the ASI.

54. Terry Manuscript, 109–10.

Chapter 4:

1. Mary Lindsey [Adolphine Fletcher Terry], *Courage!* (New York: E. P. Dutton & Co., Inc., 1938), 11.

2. Lindsey, *Courage!*, 12.

3. Terry Manuscript, 111.

4. Lindsey, *Courage!*, 24–25.

5. Terry Manuscript, 114.

6. Lindsey, *Courage!*, 9, 20.

7. Terry Manuscript, 117–118A.

8. Lindsey, *Courage!*, 92.

9. Terry Manuscript, 118B.

10. Terry Manuscript, 119–20.

11. Terry Manuscript, 120.

12. Terry Manuscript, 247.

13. Terry Manuscript, 120, 247.

14. Terry, later commissioned a second lieutenant in the infantry, was discharged on December 20, 1918, spending only six months in service. "Terry, David Dickson (1881–1963)," *Biographical Directory of the United States Congress*, http://bioguide.congress.gov/scripts/biodisplay.pl?index=T000133.

15. Joseph Carruth, "World War I Propaganda and Its Effects in Arkansas," *Arkansas Historical Quarterly* 56 (Winter 1997): 392.

16. Terry Manuscript, 123.

17. Terry Manuscript, 122–23.

18. Terry Manuscript, 125.

19. Terry Manuscript, 125–26.

20. Terry Manuscript, 126.

21. Elna C. Green, *Southern Strategies: Southern Women and the Woman Suffrage Question* (Chapel Hill: University of North Carolina Press, 1997), 6, 8.

22. Green, *Southern Strategies*, 14.

23. Mrs. T. T. Cotnam, Speech, "Women's Suffrage," circa 1918, Small Manuscript Materials, Butler Center for Arkansas Studies, Arkansas Studies Institute, Little Rock, AR; Alice (Mrs. O. F.) Ellington, "Suffrage in Arkansas," in *Suffrage in the Southern States*, comp. Ida Clyde Clarke (Nashville, TN: Williams Printing Company, 1814), 15; A. Elizabeth Taylor, "The Woman Suffrage Movement in Arkansas," *Arkansas Historical Quarterly* 15 (1956): 17–18.

24. Taylor, "The Woman Suffrage Movement," 21–22; Cotnam Speech, 1.

25. Taylor, "The Woman Suffrage Movement," 30; Carl H. Moneyhon, *Arkansas in the New South, 1874–1929* (Fayetteville, AR: University of Arkansas Press, 1997), 118.

26. Terry Manuscript, 133; Cotnam Speech, 1.

27. Terry Manuscript, 132.

28. Cotnam Speech, 2; Taylor, 31–34, 36, 42–43.

29. Taylor, 45.

30. Taylor, 49–51.

31. *Arkansas Gazette,* June 22, 1969.

32. Terry Manuscript, 133–34.

33. Peggy Harris, "'We Would Be Building': The Beginning of the Phyllis Wheatley YWCA in Little Rock," *Pulaski County Historical Review* (Winter 1995): 72.

34. Harris, "'We Would Be Building': The Beginning of the Phyllis Wheatley YWCA," 75.

35. Gail S. Murray, ed. *Throwing off the Cloak of Privilege: White Southern Women Activists in the Civil Rights Era* (Gainesville: University Press of Florida, 2004), 3–4.

36. Dorothy I. Height, "The Adult Education Program of the YWCA Among Negroes," *The Journal of Negro Education* (Summer 1945): 390.

37. Terry Manuscript, 130.

38. Marion Cuthbert, "Negro Young and the Education Program of the Y.W.C.A.," *The Journal of Negro Education* (July 1940): 363.

39. Cuthbert, "Negro Young," 363.

40. Height, "The Adult Education Program," 390.

41. Jodi Vandenberg-Daves, "The Manly Pursuit of a Partnership Between the Sexes: The Debate over YMCA Programs with Women and Girls, 1914–1933," *The Journal of American History* (March 1992): 1334.

42. Cuthbert, "Negro Young," 369.

43. Terry Manuscript, 130–31.

44. Height, "The Adult Education Program," 394.

45. Adolphine Fletcher Terry, Information Summary Sheet, Fletcher-Terry Papers, University of Arkansas at Little Rock Archives at the Arkansas Studies Institute, Little Rock, AR.

46. Terry Manuscript, 130.

47. Harris, "'We Would Be Building': The Beginning of the Phyllis Wheatley YWCA," 76.

48. Harris, "'We Would Be Building': The Beginning of the Phyllis Wheatley YWCA," 80.

49. Peggy Harris, "'We Would Be Building': A History of the Phyllis Wheatley YWCA in Little Rock," *Pulaski County Historical Review* (Fall 1996): 65.

50. Harris, "'We Would Be Building': The Beginning of the Phyllis Wheatley YWCA," 82.

Chapter 5:

1. Kenneth A. Yellis, "Prosperity's Child: Some Thoughts on the Flapper," *American Quarterly* 21 (Spring 1969): 48–49.

2. Yellis, "Prosperity's Child," 49.

3. Anne Firor Scott, "After Suffrage: Southern Women in the Twenties," *The Journal of Southern History* 30 (August 1964): 298.

4. Preston William Slosson, *The Great Crusade and After, 1914–1928*, vol. 12 of *A History of American Life* (New York: Macmillan Company, 1931), 161.

5. Scott, "After Suffrage," 299.

6. Scott, "After Suffrage," 299.

7. Scott, "After Suffrage," 301.

8. Terry Manuscript, 136.

9. Diary Kept by Adolphine Fletcher Terry, Early Years of Mary Terry and William Terry, 1914–1918, 1922, Fletcher-Terry Papers, University of Arkansas at Little Rock Archives at the Arkansas Studies Institute, Little Rock, AR.

10. Letter to Adolphine Fletcher Terry from David D. Terry, May 2, 1922, Fletcher-Terry Papers, UALR Archives at the ASI.

11. Terry Manuscript, 139.

12. Terry Manuscript, 140.

13. Terry Manuscript, 140.

14. Letter to Adolphine Fletcher Terry from David D. Terry, June 30, 1928, Fletcher-Terry Papers, UALR Archives at the ASI.

15. Letter to Adolphine Fletcher Terry from David D. Terry, July 2, 1928, Fletcher-Terry Papers, UALR Archives at the ASI.

16. Terry Manuscript, 141–42.

17. Diary by Adolphine Fletcher Terry, 1934, Fletcher-Terry Papers, UALR Archives at the ASI.

18. Terry Manuscript, 169.

19. Diary by Adolphine Fletcher Terry 1934, 19.

20. Terry Manuscript, 157–58.

21. Diary by Adolphine Fletcher Terry, 1934, 42–43.

22. Scrapbook, 1933–1937, Fletcher-Terry Papers, UALR Archives at the ASI.

23. Scrapbook, 1933–1937. As an interesting aside, in the brochure for the Women's Committee speakers, Terry listed her favorite pastime as "rough camping."

24. Gail S. Murray, "Forty Years Ago: The Great Depression Comes to Arkansas," *Arkansas Historical Quarterly* 29 (Winter 1970): 298.

25. Murray, "Forty Years Ago," 302.

26. Correspondence, 1933–1936, Fletcher-Terry Papers, UALR Archives at the ASI.

27. Diary by Adolphine Fletcher Terry, 1934, 19.

28. Terry Manuscript, 166.

29. Terry Manuscript, 166–67.

30. Terry Manuscript, 168–69; Diary by Adolphine Fletcher Terry, 1934, 29.

31. Diary by Adolphine Fletcher Terry, 1934, 84.

32. Terry Manuscript, 172.

33. Diary by Adolphine Fletcher Terry, 1934, 12.

34. Diary by Adolphine Fletcher Terry, 1934, 107.

35. Diary by Adolphine Fletcher Terry, 1934, 60.

36. American Legion Auxiliary, "Mission Outreach Committee: Americanism," http://www.alaforveterans.org/members/programs/Pages/Americanism.aspx.

37. Terry Manuscript, 159.

38. Diary by Adolphine Fletcher Terry, 1934, 5.

39. Terry Manuscript, 159.

40. Herndon, *Centennial*, 595–96, 598; Gladys McNeil, "History of the Library in Arkansas" (MA thesis, University of Mississippi, 1957), 1–4, 7; Frances Mitchell Ross, "The New Woman as Club Woman and Social Activist in Turn of the Century Arkansas," *Arkansas Historical Quarterly* 50 (Winter 1991): 339–40; Diary by Adolphine Fletcher Terry, 1934.

41. Diary by Adolphine Fletcher Terry, 1934.

42. Terry Manuscript, 161–62.

43. Hardly just an "old Ford"—according to her diary, the Terry family had three cars available during this time and mainly used them for campaigning. Diary by Adolphine Fletcher Terry, 1934, 18; Terry Manuscript, 162.

44. Diary by Adolphine Fletcher Terry, 1934, 114.

45. Booklet "Chapter XV State Libraries," Central Arkansas Library System Collection, Butler Center for Arkansas Studies, Arkansas Studies Institute, Little Rock, AR.

46. Terry Manuscript, 164.

47. Terry Manuscript, 164–65.

Chapter 6:

1. Terry Manuscript, 178.

2. Terry Manuscript, 187.

3. Terry Manuscript, 178.

4. Terry Manuscript, 180.

5. Terry Manuscript, 181–84.

6. Terry Manuscript, 185.

7. Terry Manuscript, 185–86.

8. *Arkansas Gazette*, May 9, 1971.

9. Terry Manuscript, 210.

10. Programs and Badges, 1940–1941, Fletcher-Terry Papers, University of Arkansas at Little Rock Archives at the Arkansas Studies Institute, Little Rock, AR.

11. Terry Manuscript, 214.

12. Sara Alderman Murphy, *Breaking the Silence: Little Rock's Women's Emergency Committee to Open Our Schools, 1958–1963* (Fayetteville: University of Arkansas Press, 1997), 20.

13. U.S. Department of Housing and Urban Development, "HUD History," http://portal.hud.gov/hudportal/HUD?src=/about/hud_history.

14. As quoted in Martha Walters, "Little Rock Urban Renewal," *Pulaski County Historical Review* (March 1976): 13.

15. Walters, "Little Rock Urban Renewal," 13.

16. Urban League of Arkansas, Inc., *Urban League of Arkansas, Inc. Golden Anniversary Celebration, 1937–1987* (1987): 10; Writers' Program of the Work Projects Administration in the State of Arkansas, *Survey of Negroes in Little Rock and North Little Rock* (Little Rock: Urban League of Greater Little Rock, 1941): 92.

17. Urban League of Arkansas, Inc., *Golden Anniversary*, 13.

18. Murphy, *Breaking the Silence*, 21–22.

19. Quoted in Murphy, *Breaking the Silence*, 23.

20. Murphy, *Breaking the Silence*, 24.

21. Julianne Sallee, "General Federation of Women's Clubs of Arkansas," *The Encyclopedia of Arkansas History & Culture*, http://www.encyclopediaofarkansas.net/encyclopedia/entry-detail.aspx?entryID=162.

22. Convention Minutes, April 27, 1955 and 1954–1955, Director, Arkansas Federation of Women's Clubs Collection, University of Arkansas at Little Rock Archives at the Arkansas Studies Institute, Little Rock, AR.

23. Board of Directors Meeting Minutes, September 18, 1956. Arkansas Federation of Women's Clubs Collection, UALR Archives at the ASI.

24. Terry Manuscript, 226.

25. Convention Minutes, April 26, 1957, and 1958–1960 Directory, Arkansas Federation of Women's Clubs Collection, UALR Archives at the ASI.

26. Report of the Fine Arts Department in the 1958–1960 Directory, Arkansas Federation of Women's Clubs Collection, UALR Archives at the ASI.

27. Terry Manuscript, 226–27.

28. 1958–1960 Directory, Arkansas Federation of Women's Clubs Collection, UALR Archives at the ASI.

29. Writers' Program, *Survey of Negroes in Little Rock and North Little Rock*, 60.

30. *Arkansas Gazette*, November 3, 1950.

31. Shirley Schuette, "To Serve ALL the People, 1908–1972," unpublished chapter draft, Central Arkansas Library System Collection, Butler Center for Arkansas Studies, Arkansas Studies Institute, Little Rock, AR.

32. Little Rock Library Board of Trustees Resolution, CALS Collection, Butler Center for Arkansas Studies, ASI.

33. Terry Manuscript, 227.

34. Terry Manuscript, 228.

35. Terry Manuscript, 228.

36. Shirley Schuette, "To Serve ALL the People, 1908–1972."

37. Terry Manuscript, 228–29.

Chapter 7:

1. John A. Kirk, *Redefining the Color Line: Black Activism in Little Rock, Arkansas, 1940–1970* (Gainesville: University Press of Florida, 2002), 26–31.

2. Kirk, *Redefining the Color Line*, 30.

3. Kirk, *Redefining the Color Line*, 30.

4. Lorraine Gates, "Power from the Pedestal: The Women's Emergency Committee and the Little Rock School Crisis," *Arkansas Historical Quarterly* 55 (Spring 1996): 26.

5. Johanna Miller Lewis, "Why Did It Happen Here," *Arkansas Times*, September 20, 2007.

6. Kirk, *Redefining the Color Line*, 94, 106.

7. Terry Manuscript, 230.

8. David Chappell, *Inside Agitators: White Southerners in the Civil Rights Movement* (Baltimore: Johns Hopkins University Press, 1994), 101.

9. John A. Kirk, *Beyond Little Rock: The Origins and Legacies of the Central High Crisis* (Fayetteville: University of Arkansas Press, 2007), 1.

10. Diary of Adolphine Fletcher Terry, 1958, Fletcher-Terry Papers, University of Arkansas at Little Rock Archives at the Arkansas Studies Institute, Little Rock, AR.

11. Terry Manuscript, 230.

12. Karen Anderson, "The Little Rock School Desegregation Crisis: Moderation and Social Conflict," *Journal of Southern History* 70 (August 2004): 604.

13. Terry Manuscript, 231.

14. Chappell, *Inside Agitators*, 99.

15. Grif Stockley, "Daisy Lee Gatson Bates," *The Encyclopedia of Arkansas History & Culture*, http://www.encyclopediaofarkansas.net/encyclopedia/entry-detail.aspx?search=1&entryID=591.

16. Terry Manuscript, 233–34; Sara Alderman Murphy, *Breaking the Silence: Little Rock's Women's Emergency Committee to Open Our Schools, 1958–1963* (Fayetteville: University of Arkansas Press, 1997), 56; Grif Stockley, *Daisy Bates: Civil Rights Crusader from Arkansas* (Jackson: University Press of Mississippi, 2005), 176–77.

17. Terry Manuscript, 233–34.

18. Stockley, *Daisy Bates: Civil Rights Crusader*, 177–78.

19. Terry Manuscript, 234–35.

20. Letter from Adolphine Terry to Orval Faubus, November 12, 1958, Fletcher-Terry Papers, UALR Archives at the ASI.

21. Terry Manuscript, 236–37.

22. Henry Alexander, *The Little Rock Recall Election* (New York: McGraw-Hill, 1960), 4; Chappell, *Inside Agitators*, 110.

23. Alexander, *The Little Rock Recall Election*, 4, 6; Laura Miller, *Fearless: Irene Gaston Samuel and the Life of a Southern Liberal* (Little Rock: Center for Arkansas Studies, University of Arkansas at Little Rock, 2002), 38.

24. Anderson, "The Little Rock School Desegregation Crisis," 604–5.

25. Gates, "Power from the Pedestal," 31.

26. Elizabeth Jacoway, *Turn Away Thy Son: Little Rock, the Crisis That Shocked the Nation* (New York: Free Press, 2007), 293.

27. Vivion Brewer, *Embattled Ladies of Little Rock: 1958–1963: The Struggle to Save Public Education at Central High* (Fort Bragg, CA: Lost Coast Press, 1999), 7; Murphy, *Breaking the Silence*, 71.

28. Brewer, *Embattled Ladies*, 4, 7; Murphy, *Breaking the Silence*, 70–71.

29. Gates, "Power from the Pedestal," 27, 31. Meeting Minutes, September 16, 1958, and Undated Flyer "Policy and Purpose," Women's Emergency Committee Papers, Arkansas History Commission, Little Rock, Arkansas.

30. Undated Flyer "Policy and Purpose."

31. Brewer, *Embattled Ladies*, 8–9; Murphy, *Breaking the Silence*, 68.

32. Brewer, *Embattled Ladies*, 9–12, 71–72; Murphy, *Breaking the Silence*, 72–73, 75; Resume of First Meeting, September 16, 1958, Women's Emergency Committee Papers, AHC; Stockley, *Daisy Bates: Civil Rights Crusader*, 185.

33. Terry Manuscript, 238; Brewer, *Embattled Ladies*, 9–12; Murphy, *Breaking the Silence*, 77.

34. Brewer, *Embattled Ladies*, 8–9; Murphy, *Breaking the Silence*, 68, 75; Meeting Minutes, September 23, 1958, Women's Emergency Committee Papers, AHC.

35. Murphy, *Breaking the Silence*, 79–80; Alexander, *The Little Rock Recall Election*, 6–7.

36. Meeting Minutes, September 23, 1958, Women's Emergency Committee Papers, AHC.

37. Brewer, *Embattled Ladies*, 16; Miller, *Fearless*, 42; Murphy, *Breaking the Silence*, 117.

38. Women's Emergency Committee to Open Our Schools Survey Results, Women's Emergency Committee Papers, AHC.

39. Gates, "Power from the Pedestal," 33.

40. Beth Roy, "Goody Two-Shoes and the Hell-Raisers: Women's Activism, Women's Reputations in Little Rock," in *No Middle Ground: Women and Radical Protest*, ed. Kathleen M. Blee (New York: New York University Press, 1998), 97.

41. Gates, "Power From the Pedestal," 30.

42. Murphy, *Breaking the Silence*, 87–89; Brewer, *Embattled Ladies*, 25–29.

43. Terry Manuscript, 238.

44. Brewer, *Embattled Ladies*, 15, 18; Miller, *Fearless*, 41.

45. Alexander, *The Little Rock Recall Election*, 7; Murphy, *Breaking the Silence*, 90; Miller, *Fearless*, 38.

46. Terry Manuscript, 243.

47. Chappell, *Inside Agitators*, 108, 119–20; Stockley, *Daisy Bates: Civil Rights Crusader*, 122–25; Dunbar H. Ogden, *My Father Said Yes: A White Pastor in Little Rock School Integration* (Nashville, TN: Vanderbilt University Press, 2008), 25–26.

48. These examples and others can be found in the Terry Manuscript, 240–43.

49. Alexander, *The Little Rock Recall Election*, 8–11; Brewer, *Embattled Ladies*, 56–59, 155; Murphy, *Breaking the Silence*, 172–73, 181–82.

50. Brewer, *Embattled Ladies*, 277.

51. Brewer, *Embattled Ladies*, 279–80; Murphy, *Breaking the Silence*, 232–33.

52. Letter from Sara Gibson Blanding to Adolphine Fletcher Terry, October 2, 1958, Fletcher-Terry Papers, UALR Archives at the ASI.

53. Elizabeth Jacoway, "Down from the Pedestal: Gender and Regional Culture in a Ladylike Assault on the Southern Way of Life," *Arkansas Historical Quarterly* 56 (Autumn 1997): 346; Gates, "Power From the Pedestal," 50.

54. Jacoway, "Down from the Pedestal," 351–52.

Conclusion:

1. Terry Manuscript, 250.

2. *Arkansas Gazette*, May 9, 1971.

3. *Arkansas Gazette*, July 26, 1976.

4. Terry Manuscript, 252–53.

5. *Arkansas Gazette*, June 15, 1966.

6. Harry Ashmore, "Adolphine Fletcher Terry" (speech, Adolphine Terry Dinner, Arkansas Council on Human Relations, Little Rock, AR, June 14, 1966).

7. *Arkansas Gazette*, July 26, 1976.

8. *Arkansas Gazette*, March 17, 1971; July 26, 1976.

9. Elizabeth Jacoway, *Turn Away Thy Son: Little Rock, the Crisis That Shocked the Nation* (New York: Free Press, 2007), 293

10. *Arkansas Gazette*, July 27, 1976.

11. Harry Ashmore, "Adolphine Fletcher Terry" (speech).

12. Letter to Nan from Adolphine Fletcher Terry, July 14, 1966, Fletcher-Terry Papers, University of Arkansas at Little Rock Archives at the Arkansas Studies Institute, Little Rock, AR.

Bibliography

Books

Alexander, Henry M. *The Little Rock Recall Election*. New York: McGraw-Hill, 1960.

Alford, Dale, and L'Moore Alford. *The Case of the Sleeping People: Finally Awakened by Little Rock School Frustrations*. Little Rock, AR: The Alfords, 1959.

Allsopp, Fred W., ed. *The Poets and Poetry of Arkansas*. Little Rock, AR: Central Printing Company, 1933.

Alpern, Sara, et al. *The Challenge of Feminist Biography: Writing the Lives of Modern American Women*. Urbana: University of Illinois Press, 1992.

American Association of University Women, Arkansas Division. "History, Arkansas Division, American Association of University Women." Little Rock, Arkansas: American Association of University Women, 1947.

Arkansas Department of Education. *Eighteenth Biennial Report of the Superintendent of Public Instruction of the State of Arkansas, 1903–1904*. Little Rock, AR: Central Printing Company, 1904.

Arkansas Department of Education. *Nineteenth Biennial Report of the Superintendent of Public Instruction of the State of Arkansas, 1905–1906*. Little Rock, AR: Central Printing Company, 1906.

Arkansas Department of Education. *Seventeenth Biennial Report of the Superintendent of Public Instruction of the State of Arkansas, 1901–1902*. Little Rock, AR: Central Printing Company, 1902.

Ashmore, Harry. *Civil Rights and Wrongs: A Memoir of Race and Politics, 1944–1994*. New York: Pantheon, 1994

Astin, Helen S. *Women of Influence, Women of Vision: A Cross-Cultural Study of Leaders and Social Change*. San Francisco, CA: Jossey-Bass, 1991.

Bell, Susan Groag, and Marilyn Yalom, eds. *Revealing Lives: Autobiography, Biography, and Gender.* Albany: State University of New York Press, 1990.

Bernhard, Virginia, Betty Brandon, Elizabeth Fox-Genovese, and Theda Perdue, eds. *Southern Women: Histories and Identities.* Columbia: University of Missouri Press, 1992.

Blee, Kathleen M., ed. *No Middle Ground: Women and Radical Protest.* New York: New York University Press, 1998.

Bloom, Jack M. *Class, Race and the Civil Rights Movement: The Changing Political Economy of Southern Racism.* Bloomington: University of Indiana Press, 1987.

Blossom, Virgil T. *It Has Happened Here.* New York: Harper and Brothers, 1959.

Boswell, Angela, and Judith N. McArthur, eds. *Women Shaping the South: Creating and Confronting Change.* Columbia: University of Missouri Press, 2006.

Brewer, Vivion. *The Embattled Ladies of Little Rock, 1958–1963: The Struggle to Save Public Education at Central High.* Fort Bragg, CA: Lost Coast Press, 1998.

Chambers, Erle. "Correctional Institutions." In *Arkansas and Its People: A History, 1541–1930.* New York: American Historical Association, 1930.

Chappell, David L. *Inside Agitators: White Southerners in the Civil Rights Movement.* Baltimore, MD: Johns Hopkins University Press, 1994.

Cook, Blanche Wiesen. *Eleanor Roosevelt: Volume I, 1884–1933.* New York: Viking, 1992.

Cott, Nancy F., ed. *No Small Courage: A History of Women in the United States.* New York: Oxford University Press, 2000.

Crawford, Vicki, Jacqueline Anne Rouse, and Barbara Woods, eds. *Women in the Civil Rights Movement: Trailblazers and Torchbearers, 1941–1965.* Brooklyn, NY: Carlson Publishing, 1990.

Daniel, Pete. *Lost Revolutions: The South in the 1950s.* Chapel Hill: University of North Carolina Press, 2000.

Davis, Allen F. *Spearheads for Reform: The Social Settlement and the Progressive Movement, 1890–1914.* New York: Oxford University Press, 1967.

Egerton, John. *Speak Now Against the Day: The Generation Before the Civil Rights Movement in the South*. New York: Alfred A. Knopf, 1994.

Ellington, Alice (Mrs. O. F.). "Suffrage in Arkansas." In *Suffrage in the Southern States*, edited by Ida Clyde Clarke. Nashville, TN: Williams Printing Co., 1914.

Finley, Randy, and Thomas A. DeBlack, eds. *The Southern Elite and Social Change*. Fayetteville: University of Arkansas Press, 2002.

Fowlkes, Diane. *White Political Women: Paths from Privilege to Empowerment*. Knoxville: University of Tennessee Press, 1992.

Frankenberg, Ruth. *White Women, Race Matters: The Social Construction of Whiteness*. Minneapolis: University of Minnesota Press, 1993.

Gittell, Marilyn, Isolda Ortege-Bustamante, and Tracy Steffy. *Women Creating Social Capital and Social Change: A Study of Women-Led Community Development Organizations*. New York: Howard Samuels State Management and Policy Center, 1999.

Green, Elna C. *Southern Strategies: Southern Women and the Woman Suffrage Question*. Chapel Hill: University of North Carolina Press, 1997.

Herndon, Dallas T., ed. *Centennial History of Arkansas*, vol. I. Chicago, IL: S. J. Clarke Publishing Company, 1922.

Hoeltzel, Pauline, ed. *History: Arkansas Division, American Association of University Women*. Little Rock, AR: American Association of University Women, 1947.

Huckaby, Elizabeth. *Crisis at Central High: Little Rock, 1957–1958*. Baton Rouge: Louisiana State University Press, 1987.

Jacoway, Elizabeth. *Turn Away Thy Son: Little Rock, the Crisis That Shocked the Nation*. New York: Free Press, 2007.

Kirk, John A., ed. *An Epitaph for Little Rock: A Fiftieth Anniversary Retrospective on the Central High Crisis*. Fayetteville: University of Arkansas Press, 2008.

———. *Beyond Little Rock: The Origins and Legacies of the Central High Crisis*. Fayetteville: University of Arkansas Press, 2007.

———. *Redefining the Color Line: Black Activism in Little Rock, Arkansas, 1940–1970*. Gainesville: University Press of Florida, 2002.

Ledbetter, Calvin R., Jr. *Carpenter from Conway: George Washington Donaghey as Governor of Arkansas, 1909–1913*. Fayetteville: University of Arkansas Press, 1993.

Lindsey, Mary [Adolphine Fletcher Terry]. *Courage!*. New York: E. P. Dutton & Co., Inc., 1938.

Miller, Laura A. *Fearless: Irene Gaston Samuel and the Life of a Southern Liberal*. Little Rock: Center for Arkansas Studies, University of Arkansas at Little Rock, 2002.

Moneyhon, Carl H. *Arkansas and the New South, 1874–1929*. Fayetteville: University of Arkansas Press, 1997.

Murphy, Sara. *Breaking the Silence: Little Rock's Women's Emergency Committee to Open Our Schools, 1958–1963*. Fayetteville: University of Arkansas Press, 1997.

Murray, Gail S., ed. *Throwing Off the Cloak of Privilege: White Southern Women Activists in the Civil Rights Era*. Gainesville: University Press of Florida, 2004.

Naples, Nancy, ed. *Community Activism and Feminist Politics: Organizing Across Race, Class, and Gender*. New York: Routledge, 1997.

Ogden, Dunbar H. *My Father Said Yes: A White Pastor in Little Rock School Integration*. Nashville, TN: Vanderbilt University Press, 2008.

Ostrander, Susan. *Women of the Upper Class*. Philadelphia, PA: Temple University Press, 1984.

Ryerson, Ellen. *The Best Laid Plans: America's Juvenile Court Experiment*. New York: Hill and Wang, 1978.

Schneider, Dorothy and Carl J. *American Women in the Progressive Era, 1900–1920*. New York: Facts on File, 1993.

Spitzberg, Irving J. *Racial Politics in Little Rock, 1954–1964*. New York: Garland Publishing Company, 1987.

Scott, Anne Firor. *Making the Invisible Woman Visible*. Urbana: University of Illinois Press, 1984.

———. *The Southern Lady: From Pedestal to Politics, 1830–1930*. Charlottesville: University Press of Virginia, 1995.

Stockley, Grif. *Daisy Bates: Civil Rights Crusader from Arkansas*. Jackson: University Press of Mississippi, 2005.

Terry, Adolphine Fletcher. *Cordelia, A Member of the Household*. Fort Smith, AR: South and West, Inc., 1967.

Urban League of Arkansas, Inc. *Urban League of Arkansas, Inc. Golden Anniversary Celebration, 1937–1957*. Little Rock: Urban League of Arkansas, Inc., 1987.

Wedell, Marshall. *Elite Women and Reform Impulse in Memphis, 1875–1915*. Knoxville: University of Tennessee Press, 1991.

Weeks, Stephen. *History of Public School Education in Arkansas*. Washington DC: Government Printing Office, 1912.

West, G., and R. J. Blumberg, eds. *Women and Social Protest*. New York: Oxford University Press, 1990.

Williams, Nancy, ed. *Arkansas Biography: A Collection of Notable Lives*. Fayetteville: University of Arkansas Press, 2000.

Writers' Program of the Works Projects Administration in the State of Arkansas. *Survey of Negroes in Little Rock and North Little Rock*. Little Rock: Urban League of Greater Little Rock, 1941.

Articles

Abrahams, Nancy. "Negotiating Power, Identity, Family, and Community." *Gender and Society* 10.6 (1996): 768–96.

Ackelsberg, Martha. "(Re)Conceiving Politics? Women's Activism and Democracy in a Time of Retrenchment." *Feminist Studies* 27.2 (2001): 391–419.

———. "Frances Fox Piven and the National Congress of Neighborhood Women: Grassroots Organizing." *Journal of Women's History* 14.2 (2002): 143–49.

Anderson, Karen. "The Little Rock School Desegregation Crisis: Moderation and Social Conflict." *Journal of Southern History* 70 (August 2004): 603–36.

Barnes, Paula C. "The Junior League Eleven: Elite White Women of Little Rock Struggle for Social Justice." *Arkansas Historical Quarterly* 57 (Spring 1998): 46–61.

Bartley, Numan V. "Looking Back at Little Rock." *Arkansas Historical Quarterly* 25 (1966): 47–54.

Besom, Bob. "The Springdale Meeting of the Arkansas Historical Association, 2000." *Arkansas Historical Quarterly* 59 (Autumn 2000): 311–17.

Bradley, Elizabeth. "Modern Women and Community Organization." *Journal of Educational Sociology* 23 (November 1949): 162–67.

Brown, Walter L. "Annual Meeting of the Arkansas Historical Association, 1956." *Arkansas Historical Quarterly* 15 (Winter 1956): 334–43.

Carruth, Joseph. "World War I Propaganda and Its Effects in Arkansas." *Arkansas Historical Quarterly* 56 (Winter 1997): 385–98.

Chappell, David L. "Diversity Within a Racial Group: White People in Little Rock, 1957–1959." *Arkansas Historical Quarterly* 54 (Winter 1995): 444–56.

Clemens, E. S. "Organizational Repertoires and Institutional Change: Women's Groups and the Transformation of U.S. Politics, 1890–1920." *American Journal of Sociology* 98 (1993) 755–98.

Cuthbert, Marion. "Negro Youth and the Educational Program of the Y.W.C.A." *Journal of Negro Education* 9 (July 1940): 363–71.

Daves, Jodi Vandenberg. "The Manly Pursuit of a Partnership between the Sexes: The Debate over YMCA Programs for Women and Girls, 1914–1933." *Journal of American History* 78 (March 1992): 1324–46.

Erbaugh, Elizabeth. "Women's Community Organizing and Identity Transformation." *Race, Gender & Class* 9 (2002): 8–32.

Evins, Janie Synatzske. "Arkansas Women: Their Contributions to Society, Politics, and Business, 1865–1900." *Arkansas Historical Quarterly* 44 (1985): 118–33.

Freyer, Tony A. "The Little Rock Crisis Reconsidered." *Arkansas Historical Quarterly* 56 (Autumn 1997): 361–70.

Gates, Lorraine. "Power from the Pedestal: The Women's Emergency Committee and the Little Rock School Crisis." *Arkansas Historical Quarterly* 55 (Spring 1996): 26–57.

Harris, Peggy. "'We Would Be Building': The Beginning of the Phyllis Wheatley YWCA in Little Rock." *Pulaski County Historical Review* 43 (Winter 1995): 70–86.

———. "'We Would Be Building': A History of the Phyllis Wheatley YWCA in Little Rock." *Pulaski County Historical Review* 44 (Fall 1996): 54–69.

Height, Dorothy I. "The Adult Education Program of the YWCA Among Negroes." *Journal of Negro Education* 14 (Summer 1945): 390–95.

Hood, Bobbie Sue. "The Albert Pike Home." *Arkansas Historical Quarterly* 13 (Spring 1954): 123–26.

Hudgins, Mary. "The Batesville Meeting of the Arkansas Historical Association—1967." *Arkansas Historical Quarterly* 26 (Autumn 1967): 293.

Hyde, Cheryl. "Experiences of Women Activists: Implications for Community Organizing Theory and Practice." *Journal of Sociology and Social Welfare* 13 (1986): 545–62.

Jacoway, Elizabeth. "Down From the Pedestal: Gender and Regional Culture in a Ladylike Assault on the Southern Way of Life." *Arkansas Historical Quarterly* 56 (Autumn 1997): 345–52.

Johnson, Ben F. "By Accident of Birth": John Gould Fletcher and Refashioning the Southern Identity." *Arkansas Historical Quarterly* 52 (Spring 1994): 1–18.

Kim, Mikyong Minsun. "Institutional Effectiveness of Women-Only Colleges: Cultivating Students' Desire to Influence Social Conditions." *The Journal of Higher Education* 72 (May–June 2001): 287–321.

Lisenby, Foy. "The Arkansas Conference on Charities and Correction, 1912–1937." *Arkansas Historical Quarterly* 29 (Spring 1970): 39–47.

Lisenby, Foy. "The First Meeting of the Arkansas Conference of Charities and Correction." *Arkansas Historical Quarterly* 26 (Summer 1967): 155–61.

Mancini, Olivia. "Vassar's First Black Graduate: She Passed for White." *The Journal of Blacks in Higher Education* 34 (Winter 2001–2002): 108–9.

Maxted, Mattie Cal. "Some Problems for Courts for Children in Arkansas." *Arkansas Law Review* 9 (1954–1955): 23–29.

———. "Training of Deaf Children in Arkansas." *Arkansas Historical Quarterly* 5 (Fall 1946): 193–207.

McCulloch, Rhonda E. "A Challenge to American Women." *Journal of Educational Sociology* 15 (January 1942): 301–5.

McDonough, T. James. "The Juvenile Court and Judicial Reform in Arkansas." *Arkansas Law Review* 22 (1968–1969): 17–42.

Pendergast, D'Arcy. "A Case of Agranulocytic Angina." *Canadian Medical Association Journal* 17 (April 1927).

Ross, Frances Mitchell. "The New Woman as Club Woman and Social Activist in Turn of the Century Arkansas." *Arkansas Historical Quarterly* 50 (Winter 1991): 317–51.

Scott, Anne Firor. "After Suffrage: Southern Women in the Twenties." *The Journal of Southern History* 30 (August 1964): 298–318.

Slosson, Preston William. *The Great Crusade and After, 1914–1928,* vol. 12 of *A History of American Life.* New York: Macmillan Company, 1931.

Taylor, A. Elizabeth. "The Woman Suffrage Movement in Arkansas." *Arkansas Historical Quarterly* 15 (1956): 17–52.

Walters, Martha. "Little Rock Urban Renewal." *Pulaski County Historical Review* (March 1976).

Williams, C. Fred. "Class: The Central Issue in the 1957 Little Rock School Crisis." *Arkansas Historical Quarterly* 56 (Autumn 1997): 341–44.

Yellis, Kenneth A. "Prosperity's Child: Some Thoughts on the Flapper." *American Quarterly* 21 (Spring 1969): 44–64.

Dissertations/Theses

Case, Kim. "White Women against Racism: A Qualitative Look at Anti-Racist Identity and Action." PhD diss., University of Cincinnati, 2003.

Case, Sarah Harper. "Renegotiating Race and Respectability in the Classroom: Women and Education in the New South." PhD diss., University of California at Santa Barbara, 2002.

Collins, Cathy J. "Forgetting and Remembering the Desegregation of Central High School in Little Rock, Arkansas: Race, Community Struggle, and Collective Memory." PhD diss., Fielding Graduate Institute, 2004.

Godfrey, Phoebe Christina. "Sweet Little Girls?: Miscegenation, Desegregation, and the Defense of Whiteness at Little Rock's Central High 1957–1959." PhD diss., State University of New York, Binghamton, 2001.

Hinga, Kathleen L. "Women's Local Community Activism: Paths to Politicization." PhD diss., Boston University, 2005.

Langdon, Emily Anne. "A Study of the Persistence of Affective Outcomes of Women's College Alumnae." PhD diss., University of California, Los Angeles, 1997.

McNeil, Gladys. "History of the Library in Arkansas." MA thesis, University of Mississippi, 1957.

Moyers, David Michael. "Arkansas Progressivism: A Legislative Record." PhD diss., University of Arkansas, 1986.

Rison, David Ellery, "Arkansas during the Great Depression," PhD diss., University of California, Los Angeles, 1974.

Schuyler, Lorraine Gates. "The Weight of their Voices: Southern Women and Politics in the 1920s." PhD diss., University of Virginia, 2001.

Toombs, Mrs. Kermit W. "History of Pulaski County Juvenile Administration Center." MA thesis, Arkansas State Teachers College, 1964.

Wilson, William. "History of Public School Education in Arkansas, 1900–1918." MA thesis, University of Chicago, 1918.

Papers/Manuscripts/Collections

Arkansas Association of University Women Collection. University of Arkansas at Little Rock Archives at the Arkansas Studies Institute, Little Rock, Arkansas.

Arkansas Federation of Women's Club Collection. University of Arkansas at Little Rock Archives at the Arkansas Studies Institute, Little Rock, Arkansas.

Central Arkansas Library System Collection. Unprocessed Collection, Butler Center for Arkansas Studies, Arkansas Studies Institute, Little Rock, Arkansas.

Cotnam, Mrs. T. T. Speech Given to Arkansas Legislature, 1915. Extra information added later, circa 1918. Small Manuscript Collection, Butler Center for Arkansas Studies, Arkansas Studies Institute, Little Rock, Arkansas.

Fletcher-Terry Papers. University of Arkansas at Little Rock Archives at the Arkansas Studies Institute, Little Rock, Arkansas.

Quapaw Quarter Association Records. Butler Center for Arkansas Studies, Arkansas Studies Institute, Little Rock, Arkansas.

Women's Emergency Committee Papers. Arkansas History Commission, Little Rock, Arkansas.

Online Sources

American Legion Auxiliary. "Mission Outreach Committee: Americanism." http://www.alaforveterans.org/members/programs/Pages/Americanism.aspx.

Biology Online. "Agranulocytic angina." http://www.biology-online.org/dictionary/Agranulocytic_angina.

Harris, Peggy. "Adolphine Fletcher Terry." *The Encyclopedia of Arkansas History & Culture.* http://www.encyclopediaofarkansas.net/encyclopedia/entry-detail.aspx?search=1&entryID=1779.

Pulitzer Prizes, "1939 Pulitzer Prize Winners." http://www.pulitzer.org/awards/1939.

Salle, Julianne. "General Federation of Women's Clubs of Arkansas." *The Encyclopedia of Arkansas History & Culture.* http://www.encyclopediaofarkansas.net/encyclopedia/entry-detail.aspx?search=1&entryID=162.

Stockley, Grif. "Daisy Lee Gatson Bates." *The Encyclopedia of Arkansas History & Culture.* http://www.encyclopediaofarkansas.net/encyclopedia/entry-detail.aspx?search=1&entryID=591.

United States Congress. "Terry, David Dickson (1881–1963)." *Biographical Dictionary of the United States Congress.* http://bioguide.congress.gov/scripts/biodisplay.pl?index=T000133.

United States Congress. "Terry, William Leake (1850–1917)."
Biographical Dictionary of the United States Congress.
http://bioguide.congress.gov/scripts/biodisplay.pl?index=
T000137.
United States Department of Housing and Urban Development.
"HUD History."
http://portal.hud.gov/hudportal/HUD?src=/about/hud_history.
Vassar College. "History of Vassar College."
http://historian.vassar.edu.

Newspapers

Arkansas Democrat
Arkansas Gazette
Arkansas Times

Index

About the Author

Stephanie Bayless holds a Master of Arts in public history from the University of Arkansas at Little Rock. She is a Certified Archivist and currently works in the Manuscripts Division of the Butler Center for Arkansas Studies. Bayless lives in Little Rock, Arkansas, with her husband, daughter, and son.

CPSIA information can be obtained at www.ICGtesting.com
Printed in the USA

236071LV00002B/2/P